THE
END
OF
EVIL

SUNY Series in Philosophy

Robert Cummings Neville, editor

THE END OF EVIL

Process Eschatology in Historical Context

Marjorie Hewitt Suchocki

90-2312

State University of New York Press

Published by
State University of New York Press, Albany

©1988   State University of New York

For information, address State University of New York
Press, State University Plaza, Albany, N.Y., 12246

Library of Congress Cataloging-in-Publication Data

Suchocki, Marjorie.
    The end of evil : process eschatology in historical context / by
Marjorie Hewitt Suchocki.
      p.   cm. — (SUNY series in philosophy)
    Includes index.
    ISBN 0-88706-723-9.   ISBN 0-88706-724-7 (pbk.)
    1. Good and evil.   2. Free will and determination   3. Finite, The.
4. Eschatology.   5. Theodicy.   I. Title.   II. Series.
BJ1406.S82
216—dc19   87-1934
                                                              CIP

10 9 8 7 6 5 4 3 2

for

John

Contents

Acknowledgments

The parent of this present work was itself born as a dissertation, *The Correlation Between God and Evil*, at Claremont Graduate School under the midwifery of John B. Cobb, Jr., Jack C. Verheyden, and Ekkehard Muehlenberg. All three were deeply helpful in that initial effort. After many years of John's gentle urging, I at last turned again to the topic for the purpose of revisions. The revisions, however, as is often the case with revisions, turned into a nearly total rewriting under a vision tempered and, one hopes, matured through the intervening years. Thus the present volume is the child of the first, rather than a re-presentation of the earlier work.

I am grateful for the encouragement of my editors at SUNY Press, William Eastman and Robert C. Neville, and the critical help of SUNY's readers. Also, my friend and colleague in process, Lewis S. Ford, was generous and helpful with his dialogue on those chapters dealing with process eschatology. Dr. Timothy Eastman, process physicist at NASA, gave guidance through his comments on Chapter VIII, "The Metaphysics of the Redemptive God," insofar as that chapter deals with aspects of time and space. Finally, Jack C. Verheyden once again helped with his critical evaluation of those chapters dealing with nineteenth-century theology. I am grateful for the guiding words each has given.

Introduction

In the midst of the sorrows of history, religious thinkers have sought the reason and resolution of those sorrows at the edges of history — in protology and eschatology. How is it that terror and tragedy are woven into the fabric of our lives? Can the irrational within history find a rational explanation beyond history? If the thinker can locate a reason for the problematic nature of history in a prehistorical cause, there is yet the further mystery of resolution: how is the evil thus explained to meet its end — and what, if any, is that end? Binding the two queries together is the immediate problem of how we are to understand and cope with the many dimensions of evil in personal and social history. Protology and eschatology, separated in theoretical time, are woven together as underlying assumptions in interpretations of evil within ordinary time.

The assumptions, so broadly sketched above, can be developed for personal history, for group history, or for all of history. Two basic concepts radically affect the development of these assumptions: freedom and finitude. While the two concepts are interrelated, they are not necessarily reciprocal; the freedom which can be exercised toward evil is invariably considered a finite freedom, whereas finitude may or may not entail a notion of freedom. When it does, then the tension between freedom and finitude involves the primacy accorded to one of them as the root cause of evil. Radically different interpretations of God and the overcoming of evil follow from the dominance given one concept over the other.

When freedom bears the greater weight in accounting for evil,

1

then the subjective will becomes the root cause of evil, either within history or in protohistory. Resolution to evil within history depends upon a corrected will, which becomes an anticipation of eschatological harmony. However, given the unmitigated responsibility of the subjective will in creating the problem of evil in the first place, the eschatological harmony might well entail an everlasting punishment for the recalcitrant will. The God who metes out such punishment is a God of balance and measure, of grace and judgment, acting freely from a divine will which invariably wills the good, bringing it about in God's own time.

When finitude is the primary problem, then existence is its own reason for evil, and all resolutions to evil in history are but partial triumphs against the greater tragedy of time. The finite will is but one contributor to the problem of evil, and even were that will pure, evil in the form of suffering would yet be encountered. When finite existence is viewed as created existence, then the problems for theology move into theodicy, or the justification of God in the face of unnecessary evil in creation. Atheism or reassessment of divine power and goodness then frequently crowd the theological agenda; resolution to the problem of evil hangs in the balance. Since the cause of the problem is no longer the sole responsibility of the finite will, the divided eschatology of punishment/salvation no longer addresses the problem. Evil is only fully resolved in a posthistorical universal salvation—but the notion of God, now brought into question by the primacy of finitude, may no longer provide such an eschatology.

The thesis of this work is that the contemporary era is one in which the notion of finitude is fundamental to the problem of evil—not to the exclusion of freedom, but as setting parameters that necessarily restrict the exercise of freedom. This differs from the long dominant Augustinian tradition in which the original misuse of freedom sets freedom's subsequent parameters. If we have now shifted to the primacy of finitude, then the Augustinian eschatological resolution of evil must also be revised. Evil rooted in a wayward will may be balanced eschatologically by a judgment that divides eternally, but evil rooted in finitude must be met with an eschatology of some ultimate reconciliation of all things. In the process, of course, the doctrine of God must be rigorously redeveloped.

This work studies the relation of freedom and finitude to the problem of evil as developed by Augustine and Leibniz, respectively. Having set the tension between the two concepts, we then explore the development of the problem of evil and its end in four major thinkers: Kant, who returns to radical evil in the will; Schleiermacher, who further develops the implications of evil and finitude; Hegel, who resolves evil as finitude as it is taken into the infinite; and Nietzsche, who proclaims the end to the ability to resolve the problem, save through embracing it as one's fate.

Through the philosophical categories of Alfred North Whitehead, we pick up the challenge to address the problem anew. Whitehead's concept of reality, as rhythmically both subjective and objective, allows a balanced tension between freedom and finitude whereby each conditions the other and both together provide the dynamic root of evil. Insights gained from Augustine and Leibniz, Kant and Schleiermacher, Hegel and Nietzsche, are then woven into the Whiteheadian conceptuality in order to offer a comprehensive vision of the end of evil in process eschatology.

It is also the thesis of this work that interpretations of protology and eschatology have their historical importance primarily as they influence our reasoned responses to contemporary problems. Thus the work of developing a process eschatology in historical context is not for the sake of abstract flights of fancy, nor simply to press the limits of a conceptual system of thought. Rather, formulations of reasons and ends become a shaping power of naming, energizing anew the zeal to contribute to all of earth's well-being in history's ordinary time.

I

Augustine and Liebniz:
Source and End of Evil

A ugustine and Leibniz are two of the foremost thinkers who
have respectively developed the primacy of freedom or finitude as root cause of evil. Of the two, Augustine is surely
the more fundamental; his position is aptly summarized in his phrase,
"All evil is the result of sin and its punishment."[1] While there have
been theories of the primacy of finitude throughout Christian history, not until the modern era did the notion of finitude rival
Augustine's profound explorations of evil's dependence on freedom.
Furthermore, Leibniz, one of the first great spokespersons for the
contemporary primacy of finitude, paradoxically understood himself
as developing a defense of the Augustinian position. However, his
defense actually lays bare the tensions in the Augustinian notion of
freedom, making explicit the new primacy of finitude.

The strength and power of Augustine's thought flows in no small
measure from the integrity with which he interwove his thought and
life in theological expression. But this fifth-century thinker, whose
Confessions is foremost among those writings establishing the very
genre of biography, was not one to note idiosyncratic features of
human existence. To the contrary, his interweaving of thought and
life appears to have been governed primarily by an understanding of
each human existence as a recapitulation of the fall and possible
redemption of the race. Thus he chose those features of his life for
theological reflection that illustrated the great problems of all human
existence, and, through the grace of God, the great resolution to

5

those problems as well. His *Confessions* provides an apt entry into our discussion of the subjective pole of evil, freedom of the will.

In the thirteen books of *Confessions*, the first seven illustrate the unredeemed experience of evil and its effects, while the last six explore redemption and its correction of the problem of evil. This gives a rough parallel to *City of God*,[2] where the first ten books deal with the earthly city, marked by self-love, and the last twelve deal with the contrasting heavenly city, marked by love of God. The symbolism of *Confessions*, however, is not that of two cities, but that of two trees in two gardens, with one leading to a knowledge of good and evil, and the other leading to a knowledge of life.

In Book II of *Confessions*, Augustine sets forth the famous incident of the boyhood theft at the pear tree. A comparison with the account of Adam's fall in *City of God* reveals that the theft is of no small significance in Augustine's carefully constructed story; it is, in fact, a repetition in Augustine's life of the protohistorical fall of the race in Adam. The similarities between the two accounts are striking. Augustine's theft is recorded as compelled by lust for its own sake rather than for any perceived good, since Augustine had more and better pears at home. Adam likewise possessed a great abundace of other kinds of food, so that his sin of taking forbidden fruit was also wanton. While Adam's sin was committed from a state of perfection and, therefore, without lust, it nonetheless generated lust for all the human condition, eventuating in Augustine's lustful repetition of the fall.

In yet other parallels, Augustine took the fruit for love of his companions and a desire to be in solidarity with them; Adam took the fruit "by the drawings of kindred."[3] Augustine took the fruit in pride, with an ambition to be above God, imitating "an imperfect liberty by doing with impunity things which I was not allowed to do, in obscured likeness of thy omnipotency."[4] Adam likewise fell into sin through pride, defined as "the craving for undue exaltation."[5] Lust, companionship, pride, and a falling away from God equally mark Adams's taking of the fruit and Augustine's taking of the fruit. Adam is cast forth from the garden, and Augustine concludes his own account with the statement, "I wandered too far from thee, my stay, in my youth, and became to myself an unfruitful land."[6]

The parallel between Augustine and Adam is deeply important to the position that all evil is the result of sin and its punishment. If all that is called "natural evil" in the world—affliction through fires and floods and other calamities, as well as afflictions through illness and death—follows from the misuse of the human will, and if these troubles are the lot of humankind in general, including infants and elders, rational and irrational, then clearly the personal exercise of the will is not sufficient to answer the enormity of the problem. Infants have not yet exercised their wills; how is it that some suffer death, which Augustine clearly saw to be a punishment for sin?

The question was raised acutely in Augustine's time. In *On the Deserving of Sinners and their Forgiveness*, Augustine argued that the effect of Adam's sin was such that it corrupted all his descendents, bending their wills toward self-love and, therefore, evil. Again, in *City of God* he wrote, "for we all were in that one man, since we all were that one man...already the seminal nature was there from which we were to be propagated; and this being vitiated by sin and bound by the chain of death, and justly condemned, man could not be born of man in any other state. And thus, from the bad use of free will, there originated the whole train of evil. . . ."[7] Thus the parallel in *Confessions* graphically underscores Augustine's identification with Adam. Both the bent toward sin and the exercise of sin follow from this primal identification.

If the sin of Adam accounted for the universality of sin, Augustine nonetheless had to deal with the question of why Adam, created good, fell. His answer was twofold: on the one hand, the fall had to do with the plenitude of being; and on the other, it had to do with the angelic fall and its repercussions in tempting the human will. Even though both answers could imply that finitude necessarily entails evil, Augustine absorbed this implication into the absolute primacy of the will. Clearly, he did not envision either the temporality or the mutability of finitude as in any way an evil, for he developed a position in *On the Free Choice of the Will* that plenitude requires the passing away of finite objects. This occurs as a matter of design, and not as a matter of freedom, so that this form of mutability is good. The problematic side of mutability is not its passing away, but its essential instability. Only God is fully good, because only God is fully immutable. Created beings are necessarily of a lesser good than God. Being lesser, they are therefore corruptible, some by design, as in the movements of decay within nature, and some by choice, as the deviated will. The latter, since it is contrary to its design, is wicked, while the former is not. But the very possibility of the will's wickedness would seem to be a part of its design, and hence there is room to ask Augustine whether or not mutability is in some degree the cause of the evil will.

Augustine developed the angelic fall in *City of God* by associating God's creation of the angels with God's creation of light and its separation from darkness as recounted in Genesis. Angels are considered to be creatures of light, with the separation being that of the wicked from the good. But why are some wicked? Adam's sin receives its prologue as Augustine describes a vision in which the angelic creatures, being less than God, are not in and of their own natures assured of eternal bliss, even though they are immortal. Eternal bliss follows not from immortality, but from clinging everlastingly to God, the source of all good. The mutability of the angelic orders consists in the contingency of their perseverance in good; there is no necessity in their natures whereby they *must* cling to God, and hence they are free in this regard, as Adam also will be. But it seems that God knows which angels will persevere, and which will not. Angelic happiness, however, is dependent upon assurance of forever clinging to God. Given the dependence of bliss upon the knowledge of its continuation, it would seem that those angels who know of their perseverance would be in a happier state than those who do not. For those others, anxiety over their possible fall would in fact *be* the fall. If the angel is anxious over falling away from God, then the angel's attention has turned from the immutable God to its own mutable state, and this turning is of itself a fall from its good.

From such an account, God's withholding of necessary knowledge would seem to be as essential to the fall as the created lack in the angels. Augustine is ambiguous on this point, and would surely choose not to grant it; he wavers over whether or not the good angels only receive knowledge of their eternal felicity after the wicked angels fall, or whether—as seems important to the fullness of bliss—they have possessed this knowledge from their creation. The situation implies that mutability is integrally implicated in the problem of evil, but the argument is that mutability itself is a good, which allows an evil. Augustine rests responsibility for evil in the will which misuses its mutable nature.

Having established the wickedness of Angels, Augustine then describes the order of creation, giving immortal angels superiority over the human world, where immortality depends upon persevering in fixing one's will upon the immutable God. Since there are two sources of sin, "one from man's unprompted thinking and the other by persuasion from outside,"[8] Augustine uses both to answer the question of why Adam has sinned. Adam sinned through the persuasion of the dark angel who used Adam's desire for union with his wife as a temptation, and through his own prideful lust, by which he freely chose to turn from God to his own desires.

This recounting of the fall from God, whether in Augustine, Adam, or the angels, outlines the major problem of the fallen will: It has freely chosen to turn from God toward self, which is lust—the desire for finite things in and of themselves. Lust, in turn, darkens the understanding and thus distorts knowledge. Ultimately it leads naturally to death, for lust is always directed away from God, and, therefore, away from the source of all life. Abandoned to itself, the lustful self is already spiritually dead, and is prone to illness and eventual bodily death. These are the results for Adam; they are also the results for Augustine.

We return now to *Confessions* to show Augustine's illustration of these effects of evil in his own life. The connection between lust and death is portrayed in Book IV through the death of the young Augustine's friend. The love of friendship had proved to be the most satisfying earthly love discovered by Augustine—but his friend died. The death was felt not only in its particular loss, but also in its implications for all loves directed toward a world which cannot long sustain them. The world is transient, changing, passing away—how are we to be secure in our existence? To love a friend is to place one's welfare in the welfare of the friend—but how is one's welfare to be entrusted to so insufficient a ground? The friend dies, and one is bereft; the loss is not only of the other's being, but in the other, of one's own being as well. Augustine experienced the loss of his friend in a great bitterness of soul, seeing in that death a sign of the transient nature of all existence, including his own. Yet his soul cried out for permanence—how can such longing emerge in a world so ill-suited to answer it?

The answer, of course, punctuates Augustine's account of the problem: the resolution to the corruptible, changing world is the incorruptible, immutable God. In God, Augustine claims, the soul's love is rightly directed; insofar as one loves the world through God, there is neither loss nor anxiety. However, the answer as formulated in these five chapters following the fall is given intellectually, not existentially, and as a dim apprehension of God's reality rather than as clear knowledge. This follows from the effects of lust, which interfere with true knowledge. The perverted will affects the mind, not only by keeping it tied to the creaturely knowledge of the senses, but also by clouding even sensory knowledge with a lust which distorts reality.

Love shapes knowledge; to love the changing form of things is to be caught up in a knowledge tied to the world. Again and again, Augustine attempted to escape his earthboundedness: he reasoned by degrees from the seen to the unseen; he grasped the necessity of an immutable God as the measure of the mutable world, but in every case, the knowledge of God thus attained was distant and removed. His will, so long as it tied him primarily to the transient world, was incapable of becoming that vehicle of love which could shape a correct knowledge of God and all else.

Augustine illustrated the problems of his ignorance by the puzzle which plagued him concerning the divine. Anthropomorphism appeared to him to be clearly error, yet how could he conceive of a divine substance? What is the "shape and form" of spirit? How is God present to all the world—and how is the world related to God? Finally, and in keeping with the intellectual plane of each problem, how is evil to be understood relative to God? Did God create evil? Is evil an opposing substance to the spiritual substance which is God? Once again, he poses the primary question: whence evil?

Augustine's pre-conversion answer to the question reflects the influence of Platonic philosophy. He located the source of evil in the privation of being, whereby that which is created can in no sense share the full being of the creator—else it would be of the same substance and essence as the creator. To be a creature, then, is to be created from nothing, with the concomitant tendency to fall again toward nothingness. At this point in the discussion, Augustine could name nonbeing as a source of evil; he later absorbed this into the will which actualizes evil. Augustine further followed the Platonists by placing that which we call evil within the plenitude of a universe which must manifest every form of being whatsoever—in the context of the whole universe, there is no genuine evil. Everything contributes to the harmony of the cosmic whole.

But throughout the course of his striving after a knowledge of God through the powers of his fallen intellect, there is a sense of anguish and insufficiency afflicting Augustine. His answers made rational sense to him, but left his soul unsatisfied. He concludes these books on the fallen state by remembering a time when he had lifted his mind by degrees from the seen to the unseen, from the world to God, and then saw a vision of God in the form of indescribable light. The vision is brief, a "flash of a trembling glance," but "I was not able to fix my gaze thereon; and my infirmity being beaten back, I was thrown again on my accustomed habits, carrying along with me naught but a loving memory thereof, and an appetite for what I had, as it were, smelt the odor of, but was not yet able to eat."9 Despite all the anguish of endeavor by his intellect, despite his sense of frustration in the world, he was incapable of finding release. His knowledge was not sufficient. The fault lay not in the fallen intellect alone, but in the cause of its fallenness, a misdirected and now divided will.

Insofar as the first half of *Confessions* portrays the interwoven problems of lust, death, and ignorance, it portrays the struggles which follow from the fallen will. Thus while Augustine can set the questions concerning God, evil, and redemption in these books, proper knowledge with regard to all three can come only following conversion, with its healing of the will and conferral of love, life, and knowledge. The answers to the questions he has thus far posed are not answerable by the fallen intellect. Until the will is reestablished in God, reason's power has no effect on the wellsprings of the soul. The philosophical answers given lead only more deeply to the problem of the will, a problem which finds its formulation and resolution midway in the book, in a second garden and beneath a second tree.

Augustine recounted his decision to seek knowledge through becoming a catechumen of the church. However, the closer he came to conviction of the truth of the doctrines of the church, the more hopelessly he felt himself entangled in a will which could not direct itself to be healed. That which was set in motion in the fall, first in Adam and then as reenacted by Augustine, was finally experienced in the fullness of its horror. The sin at the tree of good and evil had run full course when Augustine discovered the helplessness of a will which, enmeshed in love for the world, had not the means to lift itself to a love for God. In its division, the will is even more powerless than in its whole direction toward evil loves. Thus the soul finds itself with no means within itself for the return to God which is its redemption. Augustine captures this plight in the following significant passage:

Whence is this monstrousness? and to what end? The mind commands the body, and it obeys instantly; the mind commands itself, and is resisted.10

To will is not to be able, since the will is divided. Its very command to itself bespeaks its division and its inability to obey. If the will truly desired what it commands itself in its yearning toward God, it would need to give itself no command; it would already be that which is involved in the command. Thus the very fact of the command witnesses to a fatal falseness, a deceptiveness in the will. The result of the self-command to turn to God is, for Augustine, an agonizing recognition of an innate inability to turn. Impotent, the divided soul can only fall back on itself in despair, knowing itself captured in loves which it itself has chosen, and which it is now powerless to repudiate. There is no deliverance within the soul. Obviously, then, redemption must come from beyond the soul, from a God who actively turns the will back toward the divine.

Augustine enters the garden, steals away from his companion in order to weep, and flings himself down "how, I know not, under a certain fig-tree." In *City of God*, Christ is called the tree of life in the garden of Eden, and the shame of the guilty pair is covered by leaves taken from the fig-tree. Augustine's imagery in *Confessions* repeats this theme, showing how Augustine finds beneath one tree what was lost at that other.

Thus soul-sick was I, and tormented.... And thou, O Lord, pressed upon me in my inward parts by a severe mercy, redoubling the lashes of fear and shame lest I should again give way.... So was I speaking and weeping in the most bitter contrition of my heart, when lo! I heard ... a voice chanting, and oft repeating, "Take up and read; take up and read." ... I arose, interpreting it to be no other than a command from God to open the book. ... I read ... instantly ... by a light as it were of serenity infused into my heart, all the darkness of doubt vanished away. ... For thou converted me unto Thyself.[11]

The action of God, specifically directed toward the overcoming of the impotent will, releases Augustine from that impotence, restoring to him the ability to see and use all mutable goods in light of their relationship to that immutable good which is God.

In the remaining five chapters of *Confessions*, Augustine illustrates the triumph of God over evil, for each of the problems addressed in the earlier books is overcome. Whereas prior to his conversion he was plunged into bitterness by the death of his friend, following his conversion he piously endures four successive deaths, each one closer than the last: an acquaintance, a friend, his son, and his mother. In each case, he has loved the lost one in and through God, and can release the loved one to God. Acceptance, gratitude, and rejoicing replace bitterness.

Whereas the earlier books were pervaded with the problem of lust, Book X presents the antithesis of lust, which is the love of God and its corrective power over the vestiges of lust in the Christian soul. Finally, the problem of a true knowledge of God and creature which met such frustration in his fallen state is answered in the last four great books of the work, where Augustine's reason soars in his consideration of knowledge itself in Book X, and in his use of redeemed knowledge to explore the nature of God's good creation in the final three books.

The problem of evil, then, rests in the will which has fallen from its proper orientation toward God. The fallen will is incapable of returning to God, for it lacks the means to reestablish itself. It can no more exercise its proper function of turning to God than two broken legs can provide a person with the power of walking. Healing of the will must come from outside itself, from God alone. The experience of redemption is precisely this grace which heals the will and restores the lost gifts of creation through love and knowledge.

If this is the answer to evil in history for Augustine, what is the ultimate end of evil? The destiny of all creation is to participate in God's overcoming of evil. History, however, is but a partial manifestation of God's redemption; the fulfillment is eschatological in the City of God as it is realized eternally in the heavens. The *Confessions* alludes continually to this final fulfillment, both with its beginning appeal that our hearts are restless until they rest in God, and in the final benediction which speaks of God's own rest in that eternal Sabbath, the seventh day.

Augustine more explicitly develops the eschatological aspect of the completion of good and evil in the final three books of *City of God*. Eternal peace is the destiny of the redeemed, with a perfectly ordered enjoyment of one another and of God. The unjust likewise participate in eternal order, but with eternal wretchedness as the orderly balancing out of their sin. The redeemed enjoy eternal life, whereas the unredeemed experience eternal death. This death is particularly developed in Books XIX through XXI of *City of God*, and shows the ultimate consummation of lust. When the soul first turned from God, it lost its principle of continuance in life, for God forsook the soul. Bereft of God, the soul could not properly develop its task of governing the body. Rather, it was governed by the body's desires, lust. This first death of the God-forsaken soul culminates in the physical death of the soul-forsaken body. In the final culminaton of things, the soul and body are reunited, but now in everlasting warfare, whereby each wills the departure of the other. The soul wills the departure of the body because of the pain entailed by its presence, and the body wills the departure of the soul in order that its own sufferings might cease their consciousness. Even as lust marked the earthly existence of the unjust, even so lust is their final fate, as soul and body lust for a death to end their conflict. "Lust thou art, and to lust thou shalt return." This is the second death, but it is by definition unending, eternal.

In *On the Free Choice of the Will*, Augustine developed the thesis that the eternal misery of the damned was itself the perfection of things, for damnation provides a corrective balance to evil. Hence, "the ugliness of sin is never without the beauty of punishment."[12] He argued explicitly that the suffering of sinners is part of the perfection of the created order: "If sin occurred and unhappiness did not result from it, then evil would violate order . . . when sinners are unhappy, the universe is perfect."[13] Here the plenitude of being is served, for the harmony of the universe is maintained by each grade of being fulfilling its destined place eternally. The creator God brings creation to its completion through redemption and damnation. Both are enacted in history, receiving their culmination in eternity. The Christian understanding of the root of evil generated from the free choice of the will found its redemptive resolution in the final eschatological harmony of creation, predestined by the immutably redemptive God.

In this consideration of the source and end of evil developed around the centrality of the fallen will, the Adamic and angelic protology and the posthistorical eschatology of justice create boundaries for history, and hence allow history to become itself. Life is a small drama set within a much wider context; the nonhistorical parameters of time turn time into a story moving steadily toward its denouement. The wayward will is the tension within the story which provides its dramatic motif.

Alongside this dominant story within the Christian tradition is another that associates evil less with the subjective will than with the objective conditions of finitude. To associate evil with finitude, however, raised the vexing problem of divine responsibility. A path beyond such an unacceptable conclusion was to view evil not as unmitigated, but as an ultimately positive force in creation. Irenaeus,

Lactantius, and Clement of Rome are among those who suggested that evil may be necessary as the opportunity for growth and goodness, and, therefore, not incompatible with God's creative goodness. However, such formulations were overshadowed by the Augustinian theory that free will rather than creatureliness was the fundamental source of evil. The Augustinian notion held sway for a thousand years, despite changes in nuance and interpretation of the effects of evil.

In the seventeenth and eighteenth centuries, however, a major philosophical shift occurred that reintroduced the importance of finitude itself as necessarily implicated in evil. The modern philosophers were preoccupied with the nature of things as they are, not as they ought to be or will become. What had been was counted as more reliable than what will be for understanding the world, and efficient causation replaced the long domination of final causation.[14] Whether initiated through the empiricism of Francis Bacon, the physical analysis of Newton, or the methodological doubt of Descartes, the modern temper generated a philosophical skepticism toward any principle not immediately inferrable from the data at hand. What could be inferred was considered to be laws of motion, geometric truths, and distinctive realms of extension on the one hand, and rationality on the other. The most critical difference for our consideration was the shift from an emphasis on immutability and mutability as the primary distinction between God and creature to the prominence of infinity and finitude as the central distinction. Immutability and mutability were generally retained as categories, but they no longer played the decisive role given them by Augustine. In their place was a sense of the utterly unlimited nature of deity, and the contrasting limitations which mark finite existence.

When mutability is superseded by finitude as the distinctive characteristic of creaturely being, a problem arises with reference to the cause of evil. So long as the focus is on mutability, the creature appears able to assume responsibility for its turn away from the good; the problem is in the creature's choice, not in the creature's nature. Hidden within this responsibility, however, is the ambiguity of a mutable nature which undermines the capacity to remain fixed upon the good. Only insofar as the creature is reinforced with grace can it remain as it should be. Since this grace must come from God, the turn of the creature toward evil indicates insufficient grace from God, in which case the line of responsibility is blurred. In the overwhelming emphasis upon mutability and the turning will in the Augustinian formulation, this problem remained implicit.

However, the modern preference for the category of finitude turned attention away from the will alone to the condition of nature. Causes of moral evil were sought in natural or necessary conditions such as climate, society, geography, and laws of matter. Finitude per se, rather than the turning will exclusively, became for many the domain in which to investigate the causes of evil.

Pierre Bayle was perhaps the most vociferous exponent of the consequent thought that sin, rather than being the cause of evil, is caused by prior evil conditions. For Augustine, the human experience of natural events as evil was a direct result of sin, whereas for Bayle, the experience of natural evil was conducive to human sinning. The priority was reversed. In his enormously popular *Dictonnaire historique et critique*, to which Leibniz responded with the *Theodicy*, Bayle repeatedly argued that sin is an irrationality, part of the givenness of things in the world, and that no doctrine of God can account for the presence of such evil without implicating God in responsibility.[15] Evil, belonging to the structure of the world as we find it, gave no evidence of being a penalty imposed for the sin of a first erring man, but instead gave evidence that there is an ultimate dualism of good and evil which extends to the principles which account for the existence of the world. Finitude, weakness, irrationality—all are involved in the existence of evil as well as good in this world, so that the onus of evil is no longer borne entirely by the turning will. If nature itself was essentially flawed, so that it could not refrain from evil, then how could the creature be held responsible for that which could not be avoided? Would not the creator of that finite creature bear the final responsibility for evil? The question of theodicy emerged in the foreground of modern thought.

G. W. Leibniz is a natural choice for an exploration of the shift away from the Augustinian conception of evil and its end precisely because in many ways, Leibniz saw himself as a defender of Augustine. However, an analysis of his work shows his own shift to finitude, along with a corollary change in the eschatological resolution to evil.

Throughout Augustine's writings, "unchangeable" was repeatly used with the name of God, and "mutable" constantly qualified creaturely being. But these qualities were seldom utilized by Leibniz; in their place are references to the infinite and the finite. For Augustine, immutability functioned as the guarantee of the indestructibility necessary to the conception of God; but for Leibniz, infinity served this role of guaranteeing deity because of the relation between infinity and possibility. He understood possibility to be a dynamic urge toward existence, hindered only by the contradictions and incompatibilities of finitude. But God, if God be possible, is also infinite, and, therefore, confronts neither contradiction nor incompatibility. With no barrier to existence, God must necessarily exist.[16]

Infinity not only accounted for the existence of God, it also dominated Leibniz's understanding of divine perfection, that ancient consideration of the excellence of God which Augustine once called the most common definition of God. Unlike Augustine, Leibniz did not emphasize perfection as simplicity and unity. Rather, he emphasized perfection as qualities which admit of infinitude, such as power, knowledge, and will, which is also named as goodness.[17]

Such qualities have no limitations or restrictions of applicability in themselves. And yet, unified in the one nature which is God, power, knowledge and will intermingle in such a way that they produce limitation of choice.[18] Each attribute influences the exercise of the others, so that Leibniz can speak of a derivative attribute of justice, which is the powerful exercise of God's goodness in conformity with wisdom.

The quality of justice, derived from the notion of God's infinity of perfection, became the final causation of all God's activity, accounting for creation, evil, and redemption through the principle of preestablished harmony. God, knowing all possibilities for existence, both in the things themselves and in the infinite variety of interrelationships obtainable through the various combinations of possible existences, selects the one combination which can produce the greatest variety along with the greatest order. This selection by God is the crucial preestablished harmony which then governs the entire order of created being. The preestablished harmony acts as both protology and eschatology in Leibniz, since it determines both the source and the end of the world. It is, in its far-reaching effects, an eternal decision encompassing all temporal events.

In *Principles of Nature and Grace*, Leibniz describes the created nature of the world as a myriad of internally active units, or monads. These monads are without parts and are indivisible and indestructible; their activity is explained in terms of their perceptions and appetition. Since monads are internally self-contained, these perceptions and appetitions do not depend upon the external world, even though they are compatible with that external world. Leibniz understood the monads to be "windowless," having their responses contained everlastingly in the individuality of each unique monad.

These ultimate substances combine and intermingle in such a way that the entire universe is nothing other than their harmonious interaction. Conversely, the inner activity of each monad is a microcosm reflecting the entire universe. Each monad can be considered a unique perspective on the entire actual world, so that the universe is mirrored in as many ways as there are monads. The monads are thus both an ultimate diversity and an ultimate harmony—they make up a universe. While Leibniz explains the diversity through the windowless structure of monadic being, whereby each entity is independent of the other structurally, his explanation of the harmonious interaction of the monads depends upon preestablished harmony. The harmonious interaction of each monad with all others is built into its nature from the perspective of an ultimate cause which has itself envisioned the most desirable interaction possible.[21]

God as the principle of sufficient reason has introduced moral considerations for the actualization of this world, considerations which are integral to the notion of preestablished harmony. This moral structure underlies the physical structure of the world, since ultimately it is the moral structure which has made just these physical actualities existent. Through God's creative decision, individual monads are given existence according to their ultimate contributions to the desired pattern. The monads, though "windowless" themselves, are everlastingly adjusted to the motions of their fellow-designated existents.

Leibniz referred to both the individuality and the totality of created being as a perfectly automated and animated machine.[22] Just as a portion of any machine cannot be judged properly unless one knows its function in the entire mechanism, even so the meaning of any monad depends ultimately upon its relationship to the entire universe. This relationship requires not only a temporal reference but an eternal one; it is not sufficient to know how a thing is related at one point of time or space to the universe in order to pronounce a qualitative judgment on that event, for the monad contains a relationship to all of time. The whole of creation is required for an adequate assessment of the monad's worth; the end of time must be known in order to evaluate any portion therein. The entire context is the universe, in all of its dimensions. Apart from this, no judgment is complete.[23]

The preestablished harmony, then, refers not only to the inter-actions of all monads at any given point in time and space,[24] but to the more encompassing totality of all times and all spaces whatsoever. This is the realm of grace, the final sufficient reason for which God has actualized a universe. The preestablished harmony lies within the justice of God, as God's wisdom forsees the optimum good which divine power can bring forth. Upon such grounds, "the actual existence of the best that wisdom makes known to God is due to this, that His goodness makes Him choose it, and His power makes Him produce it."[25]

How does evil fit within this schematism? The preestablished harmony requires that the evil which we observe and experience is necessary to the very nature of harmony. In this notion there are echoes of Augustine; but Leibniz, more than Augustine, must somehow show that evil is necessary to the good. The preestablished harmony must be such that the world would be less than perfect were evil not included; only thus is this the "best of all possible worlds." This introduces the need to argue that God, though the author of preestablished harmony, is not morally responsible for evil.

Leibniz dealt with the problem by arguing for the freedom of the monadic essences. He understood these essences as spontaneous activity, and in the case of monads with high degrees of rationality, he saw this activity as a reflection of God's activity, or as action conformed to the monadic perception of the best possible course. Each rational monad could imitate God, thus conforming to the supreme rationality through its own limited perception of the rational order. Thus monads which are rational spirits participate knowingly in the preestablished harmony, and belong to the moral order of being, the kingdom of grace. This is their sphere of freedom.

This sphere of freedom, however, is a determined freedom. Each monad is eternally self-contained—"windowless"—acting according to the essence which it has always been potentially, and now actually through the creative act of God's will.[26] How, then, did Leibniz see this determined freedom as responsible freedom?

In *Discourse on Metaphysics*, Leibniz considered the problem through the case of Judas, the betrayer of Jesus.

Whence comes it then that this man will assuredly do this sin? The reply is easy. It is that otherwise he would not be a man. For God foresees from all time that there will be a certain Judas, and in the concept or idea of him which God has, is contained this future free act. The only question, however, which remains is why this certain Judas, the betrayer who is possible only because of the idea of God, actually exists. To this question, however, we can expect no answer here on earth excepting to say in general that it is because God has found it good that he should exist notwithstanding that sin which he foresaw.[27]

Judas is responsible for his actions; God is responsible for actualizing the Judas who will commit those actions, for reasons relating to the preestablished harmony.

However, the responsibility of Judas for his actions is strange, particularly when understood in light of the closing pages of the *Theodicy*.[28] In the Leibnitian consideration of an infinite number of possibilities, there are infinite variations on the theme of every essence. There would be, then, in the many ideas which God has of a possibly existing Judas, a variation which freely refrains from the betrayal. Hence there are a myriad possible Judas monads, each of which acts differently to some degree from all other Judases. And yet these Judases are possibilities only, ideas, potentialities pressing toward existence, awaiting the power of God's will to unleash the limitations which hold them in non-being. Whichever possible Judas is actualized will be one which acts according to the essence which it has contained eternally in the state of possibility. Its action flows from the particular variation which that essence represents on the "Judas" theme. It is, therefore, free—and so would be the actions of every other variant Judas. For Leibniz, this makes Judas himself, and not God, the one who is responsible for what he does.

And yet if this actualized monad is indeed to be responsible, then the responsibility must be traced to his "idea." Can an "idea" be responsible? The existent Judas may be the actualization of the idea, but since the existent Judas had nothing to do with either the idea or its entrance into history, how is he responsible for the variation he represents?

If all variations are necessary, so that a betraying Judas must be included as a possible variation along with all others, then responsibility would seem to rest with the one selecting the existent variation. If Judas himself were free to survey the possibilities for his life, and from these possibilities select betrayal, then Judas would appear to be the responsible agent. But the possibilities are not really open to the existent Judas. The freedom which Leibniz wished to assign to the existent Judas who acts according to his predetermined nature is better described as a mythical freedom belonging to the equally mythical ideal Judas, which might be construed as the aggregate of all the possible natures which could conceivably belong to him. Since the existent Judas is not a composite of all the Judas possibilities, but only the embodiment of one preexistent idea, then it is difficult to see any true responsibility accruing to him. The one who selects from among all the possibilities just this one, with these actions, would appear to be responsible—and that one is God, acting in conformity with divine goodness and wisdom.

If God, in actualizing the Judases of the world, has in fact brought evil into existence, these evils in combination with numerous other monadic existences constitute the most harmonious existence possible. The total harmony of the whole is the overcoming of the evil of the constituent parts. The good which is served through each particular evil is such that the entire universe is better than it would have been without each evil. "O felix culpa" rings throughout the Leibnitian notion of evil in relation to the preestablished harmony. Indeed, in choosing the paradigm case of Judas, Leibniz has chosen happily, since of course it is just that particular evil which inaugurates the events of the Christian era. Judas illustrates the use which evil may serve toward a greater good, thereby demonstrating that a harmony may be achieved not only despite evil but because of evil. Projected to the cosmic level, the "best of all possible worlds" is possible precisely because of the evils as well as the goods which have gone into its becoming. Final causation, the preestablished harmony, is the ultimate reason for evil.

Like Augustine, Leibniz utilized the notion of the City of God, seeing it as synomous with the preestablished harmony. But there is a profound difference in the Leibnitian usage of the concept which appears to relate to the infinitude/finitude theme so important to Leibniz. The City of God is no longer simply the society of the redeemed, existing alongside a contrasting earthly city; it is now the entire realm of rational spirits. Whereas Augustine divided people according to their loves, thus making the City of God the separation of human beings, Leibniz makes no such distinction.

For Leibniz, the distinction is one in which nature and grace refer to the gradation of beings in the world, such that those which are nonrational, governed primarily by efficient causaton, belong to the physical world of nature, and those which are rational and hence influenced particularly by final causation, belong—all of them—to the realm of grace, which is the City of God. This City is none other than the universe considered as the manifestation of God's own choice of final causation, the preestablished harmony. Creaturely reflection of this final causation is participation in the moral universe and active exercise of citizenship in the City of God. But since all rational spirits exercise the faculty of final causation, all likewise reflect and participate in this realm of grace: the City of God is thus composed of all rational spirits. It is not a division, but rather an inclusion of all in the moral universe in the sphere of grace.

The cosmic harmony maintained by Augustine utilized an eternal division of the two cities of the saved and the damned. For Leibniz, both the saved and the damned are incorporated into the one eternal City. This is not to say that Leibniz differs from Augustine in the consideration of punitive justice balancing evil, for here he follows adamantly the Augustinian path. There are those within his City of God who are destined for eternal punishment; this is the main-tenance of harmony on the principle that punishment balances guilt. For Leibniz, the guilt is an eternally persistent attitude, and, therefore, the punishment is likewise eternal. This balance contrib-utes to the cosmic harmony within the City, and is in keeping with the finite beginning of evil: God has actualized those evils insofar as they serve the consequent best; they become "happy faults," and, therefore, they serve in their own way in the final greatest perfection. Their inclusion in the City of God, albeit in so negative a sense, simply demonstrates their necessity to the total system.

Contrarily, the sharp division of the cities in Augustine seems more in keeping with his emphasis upon the mutability of the creature, and the turning will as the source of evil. In mutability, unlike finitude, the voluntary choice of the creature is in the foreground of consideration, regardless of the ultimate problem which lurks beneath the cloak of predestination, rendering responsi-bility for evil as problematic as it is in the notion of finitude. Given this more apparent connection of evil with a fallen will, exclusion from the City of God follows. The damned earthly city, in its eternal torment, represents a self-exclusion from the celestial blessedness. This is in keeping with the Augustinian confinement of responsibility to the will rather than to the nature of the creature. Leibniz, not Augustine, addresses himself to a theodicy.

But there is a further consideration to be derived from Leibniz's placement of evil within the confines of the realm of grace, even though Leibniz himself did not move in the direction we propose. If the evil is compensated by its overcoming within the City of God, is there not the suggestion here that there could be a positive, as well as negative, participation in the final harmony? The very incorporation of the evil within that eschatological realm means that evil is in the sphere of redemption. In the interrelationship of all things, the evil has helped to create the good and has its own contributory place in the scheme of things. By therefore including even the evil of rational spirits within the City of God, Leibniz offers the suggestion of a more positive dimension to the end of evil than does Augustine. Finally, what Leibniz has done is to take up that evil which has stemmed from the finitude of being, and place it in a City which originates in the infinity of God.

Leibniz has told us that the true meaning of events must be judged in the total context of the event, and that the total context is the entire universe in all its dimensions, historical and eschatological. Does not this wider context change the meaning of the evil? By his retention of an eternal guilt and punishment in the harmony, Leibniz evidently does not want to carry this change of meaning to the point where the evil itself is turned to good rather than balanced by good. However, his inclusion of the finite in the infinite context would seem to allow the possibility of the more radical overcoming of evil. For if the infinite takes the finite into itself, utilizing and overcoming its evilness in harmony, does not that evil become a participant in good? If a participant, does that evil then become good? Can the infinite transform and so redeem the finite? Leibniz, with his inclusive City of God, allows the questions, while Augustine, with his two exclusive cities, does not.

It is notable that in discussing the overcoming of evil in Leibniz we have had to focus on the eschatological dimension of the City of God. This is not at all because Leibniz excludes any temporal application of the notion of harmony; on the contrary, the moral universe is continually operative in a harmony whereby "nature itself leads to grace, and grace, by the use it makes of nature, brings it to perfection."[29] Worked out in time, this translates to a life which is ordered by the perception of the rational order of the universe, enjoying that order in the praise of its Author and Master. Justice, exercised in the finding of "pleasure in the perfections and the felicity of the beloved,"[30] follows one's earthly way when one lives in conformity to the laws of the moral universe.

Thus temporal answers to evil are surely found in Leibniz, actualized according to the preestablished harmony. When that preestablished harmony seems too much a matter of faith and not enough a matter of sight, the fault is with our limited perception, our finite inability to perceive the fullness of the final harmony. This final harmony, which is the eschatological dimension of the City of God, is the only sure appeal for the overcoming of evil. The perversion of nature in a turned will, and the divine turning of the will back to God which is the foundation of Augustine's City of God, is far less prominent for Leibniz, replaced by a finite order which is, eschatologically, as perfect as possible.

By using the infinite/finite distinction—not to the negation of the immutable/mutable, but certainly to its overshadowing[31]-Leibniz has spoken of evil and its overcoming in categories which had become important in his day. In many respects, despite his differences, he has adapted to Augustinianism. His major answer to evil, the preestablished harmony, is equivalent to predestination. In the process of developing his own version of this, Leibniz revealed the implicit threat in Augustine, which is the question of a divine responsibility for evil. The formulation of an answer to such evil on the basis of infinity, while it reveals the problem, does not adequately solve it owing to the insufficiency of the establishment of the creaturely freedom. Failure to resolve this difficulty leads inexorably to the unacceptable conclusion that the God who overcomes evil is the God who causes evil. Yet if God causes evil, then good and evil are both rooted in eternity/infinity, in which case there is no assurance that evil is ever finally overcome.

Both Augustine and Leibniz have interpreted evil according to dominant philosophical categories of mutability and finitude respectively. Leibniz illustrates the shift from freedom of the will to finitude itself as the source of evil, and the tension which results in trying to deal with the reality of freedom and the content of redemption. If God created conditions which necessarily entail evil, the eternal punishment as the correction of evil seems a dubious justice. With Leibniz's pseudo-defense of the Augustinian position, the two poles of evil are both clearly established, and the tension between them will mark all subsequent theology.

II

Kant and Schleiermacher: Freedom and Finitude

In Augustine and Leibniz, the subjective and objective poles of evil were given profound expression; freedom and finitude set the parameters of evil's origin. The poles are interrelated in each writer, but the dominance shifted from freedom to finitude. With the shift, the expression of the end of evil likewise changed shape. Insofar as finitude played a greater role in the existence of evil, implications were raised concerning the responsibility of God and the nature of evil's end.

Eighteenth-century responses to Leibniz's *Theodicy* were largely positive, but the tensions within the work surfaced through Immanuel Kant's *On the Failure of all Attempted Philosophical Theodicies*, published in 1791. Thereafter Kant, in *Religion Within the Limits of Reason Alone*, developed his own profound analysis of the origin and end of evil, as did his younger contemporary, Friedrich Schleiermacher.

Kant and Schleiermacher show particular affinities with Augustine and Leibniz, respectively, but with differences significant enough to mark a changed perception of evil inaugurating the contemporary era. Immanuel Kant wrote his philosophy primarily as a clarification of the limitations and uses of reason, addressing the great theme of the Enlightenment in his powerful Critiques. With regard to the subject of evil, his early works conform to the general Enlightenment opinion, manifested particularly in Leibniz, that this indeed is the best of all possible worlds. Evil serves rational purposes, and, therefore, is itself within the realm of rationality. "The whole is for the best, and everything is good in relationship to the whole," he wrote as his concluding statement in *An Attempt at Some Considerations on Optimism* in 1759.

By 1764, however, Kant had encountered the troubling works of Rousseau, bespeaking the deeper complexities of human nature. Human freedom moved more centrally into Kant's deliberations, with tension developing between freedom and nature, history and destiny. The teleological optimism of his earlier work began to crumble.

In *Critique of Judgment* (1790), Kant carefully developed rules which circumscribe the use of the concept of purpose in nature and history. This was followed in 1791 with his small essay, *On the Failure of All Attempted Philosophical Theodicies*, in which he categorized the varying possibilities for justifying God in light of moral and physical evil. Teleology had formed a cornerstone for theodicy; Kant systematically argued the insufficiency of the varying forms of the teleological argument, since it presumes more knowledge than is given the finite condition. He concluded the essay with the story of Job. The only valid response to the mystery of evil is finally the honest recognition of one's own limitations of knowledge and action. To attempt a theodicy is to claim more knowledge than is possible within finitude, so that theodicy is finally a matter of faith. In the "Concluding Remarks" of the article, Kant argued for sincerity and simplicity of conscience, setting this argument in the midst of a consideration of malice, worthlessness, and a universal duplicity in the depths of the human heart.

Thus he set the stage for his monumental assertion and investigation of "radical evil" in *Religion Within the Limits of Reason Alone*, published in 1793.[1] Given the Enlightenment interpretation of evil as following upon the natural conditions of the world, with sin being but the human manifestation of evil inherent in a difficult universe, Kant's formulation of the problem as radical and as rooted solely in human freedom came as a profound shock.

Kant's restatement of the understanding of evil followed from his analysis of human nature in *Religion Within the Limits of Reason Alone* into three predispositions.[2] Kant carefully considered human nature first in its animality, which involves self-preservation, propagation of the species, and communal impulses; then in its humanity, which he saw as the rational ability to compare one's condition with that of others; and finally in its personality, which is accountability due to the capacity for respecting the moral law. The vices which accrue from a misuse of these natural propensities account for all actual deeds of evil, yet it must be noticed that these vices can only be pronounced so by the third requirement of human nature, the predisposition to personality.

Kant lists as perversions of human animality the vices of gluttony, lasciviousness, and lawlessness; but since these vices are not contradictions of the predisposition, but merely the extreme development of it, they cannot be pronounced evil within the realm of sheer animality alone. Gluttony is not necessarily a hindrance to self-preservation, nor does lasciviousness prevent propagation of the species. Lawlessness presupposes community, and hence could easily be considered as a variation within it. The same could be said of the vices concerning the predisposition to humanity—the vices of jealousy and envy do not negate the capacity to compare oneself with others, but are simply products of comparison. Thus the analysis of human nature into animality and humanity does not yet establish the extreme development of these predispositions as vices; this task can only be done by the third element of human nature, the accountability which comes from the capacity to respect a moral law which appears to be imposed upon human nature as the decree of its just limitations.[3] The recognition of evil is a judgment upon a misuse of nature that is not itself derived from nature. This capacity for such recognition constitutes the uniqueness of human personality.

Having thus analyzed human nature in terms of these three predispositions, all of which are good, Kant declared human nature itself good. How is it, then, that human beings transgress so universally the boundaries of nature given to them? Whence evil? No less than Augustine, Kant had to address the question of the misuse of the will in a nature which is essentially good. Like Augustine, Kant's answer locates evil in the freedom of the will, but unlike Augustine, he needs no recourse to Adam or angelic orders. In his analysis, the human will is in itself sufficient to account for evil. He considered the capacity to know the moral law through the predisposition to personality as a sufficient reason for establishing that one ought to know that law and one's limits, and thus act accordingly: potentiality establishes responsibility. This potentiality is as yet a deficiency, a capacity awaiting development—the lack, however, is not an evil. To act without recourse to the rule—an inevitability, since the capacity awaits development—is an immediate plunge into evil. It is to give way to the sensuous desires of the first two predispositions without regard to the just limitations of the moral law. To do so is to undercut the ground of one's basic humanity, since to be fully personal is to exist as the integrated unity of the three predispositions, under the governance of the third. Thus to act on the basis of the desires of the first two alone is to act against one's nature, or to corrupt one's nature. Therefore, the existential nature of humanity, acting without reference to the moral law, is one of radical evil.

How is this evil overcome? There is some ambiguity in Kant's answer. On the one hand, he stressed that the presence of a law implies the ability to fulfill that law:[4] the capacity within one for the highest maxim is not only a limitation of one's nature, but a call to live within these limitations in dutiful obedience to the highest law. The sensuous inclinations leading to an extravagant use of nature must—and, therefore, can—be brought into obedience to the moral imperatives. On the other hand, he spoke of evil as so radical that it is "inextirpable by human powers."[5] This follows from the continual failure to act in accordance with the rule, hence building up within the self a propensity not toward the good but toward the evil principle. The human will becomes corrupt, and here indeed there are echoes of Augustine. However, for Kant, the corruption is never absolute; the corrupt will cannot annihilate its capacity to apprehend the moral law, since this capacity belongs to its very nature, and is in fact its freedom. The constant presence of this capacity is the key to overcoming evil.

The role of God in this overcoming relates to the transcendent element of the moral law noted earlier. One might say that while evil may find its account wholly within human nature, the good cannot. God is that Holy Lawgiver, that Supreme Being whose idea of moral perfection issues into a creation where that perfection can be manifested. The fundamental mode of this manifestation is the predisposition to personality, with its capacity to subordinate all desires to the desire for goodness alone. In this sense, every human being is made in the image of God. Thus the capacity for the moral law is at once human and divine: human, as a predisposition essential to our nature, and divine insofar as the exercised capacity is an incarnation of that idea which proceeds from God's very being.[6] Then the person is indeed a "Son of God." The role of God in overcoming evil, then, is essentially connected with this dual aspect of the moral law: its actuality in God, and its potentiality in humankind.

There are two routes toward overcoming evil. The one results from the innate power of the idea of the moral law alone; the other results from the power of example as the moral law is actualized in history. The power of the idea alone is captured in the following:

Yet there is one thing in our soul which we cannot cease from regarding with the highest wonder, when we view it properly, and for which admiration is not only legitimate but even exalting, and that is the original moral predisposition itself in us.[7] . . .

Now it is our universal duty as men to elevate ourselves to this ideal of moral perfection, that is, to this archetype of the moral disposition in all its purity —and for this the idea itself, which reason presents to us for our zealous emulation, can give us power.[8]

However, the innate power of the idea is dulled to one's perceptions by the habituated disposition to evil; this is the sense in which evil is "inextirpable by human powers." The problem is not unlike that encountered by Augustine in his formulation of freedom as the source of evil. For Augustine, the perverted will might grasp the good, even as Augustine did in his vision of God in Book VII of *The Confessions*. But the recognition of the good is not sufficient—he fell again. The turned will does not have the power within itself to return to God, despite its capacity to recognize and long for the good. The ambiguity in Kant is that on the one hand the ability to see and desire the good is already the correction of the will, but habituated evil weakens this ability. Note, however, that evil does not—cannot— eradicate this ability. In a sense, his problem is to find a way to increase the corrupted will's openness to the good, without recourse to a debilitating grace which substitutes God's actions for one's own.

The second aspect of the moral law, its power through its incarnation in another, is the means whereby the will is awakened to the innate power of the moral law within itself. The example of the other calls us to ourselves, releasing the innate power of the idea. This creates a desire that this holy principle might be our highest maxim so that we might always act by this rule. A disposition toward good for its own sake then fosters actions in accordance with the rule. The good intention is itself the primary thing, even though within the frailty and complexity of finitude it will always be a struggle to actualize the intention.

The problem with this second route, of course, is the regress involved. If the power of an example in another is sufficient to awaken the will to its own capacitites, how does that first example come to be? What accounts for the break in the chain of radical evil? Kant's account skirts this problem with use of language that evokes Christian sensibilities concerning Christology. The implication is that God provides the needed example through the particularity of Jesus, so that the power of his example is sufficient to awaken others. These others then form a community of like-minded individuals, so that the example of Jesus is both retained in a written witness and in the perpetuated living witness of those awakened to the holy maxim. Kant's language, however, is evocative and implicatory, not explicit. He focuses upon the effects of the example, not upon how that example is possible given an otherwise universal propensity to evil. To do so would have involved him more centrally in the issue of grace.

Kant deeply resisted the notion of grace, seeing it as a dangerous substitute for one's own efforts to moral action. Grace is essentially the action of another, not of ourselves, but the good is defined by Kant as precisely entailing action by ourselves. He eschews grace as being either an incomprehensible and, therefore, nondiscussable possibility beyond the reaches of reason, or else as a dangerous superstition whereby we avoid the call to responsibility in moral action, waiting instead for a miraculous intervention which will accomplish our betterment of character without any painful effort on our own part.[9] If grace were this, then in principle it could not be effective—it would violate the nature of the good, and human nature as well. But there is an operating notion of grace in Kant's depiction of the overcoming of evil, both through the provision of at least one example of the incarnate moral law within history, and through the presence of the moral law itself. In sentences ringing with reminders of the medieval merits of condignity and congruity associated with grace, Kant describes the progress of the individual gripped by the power of the moral law. This grace releases the power of the archetype despite habituated evil, counts the intention to good as righteousness even when the resultant act is only a mixed good, and counteracts the lingering power of one's former life of evil. In this sense, God is the power that releases the human power for good.

Through the power thus given, our fundamental intentions are changed; and though the actualization of these intentions in daily conduct is a slow and sometimes painful affair of varying degrees of success and failure, the intention itself counts for the deed—and this Kant does call grace. Through the attractive power of the archetype released within us, the disposition to evil is overcome. Progress is particularly evident in the ethical commonwealth, the "union of hearts," where the moral law manifests its social character.

In Books I and II of *Religion Within the Limits of Reason Alone*, Kant deals with evil primarily in terms of the individual will. However, since the essence of the moral law is a fundamental equity in society, whereby self-interest is subordinated to the interests of all, the good itself is necessarily social. Book III and IV treat the social aspects of goodness in ideal and historical form. The well-intentioned individual must become aligned with a community of like-minded persons.

... the highest moral good cannot be achieved merely by the exertions of the single individual toward his own moral perfection, but requires rather a union of such individuals into a whole toward the same goal—into a system of well-disposed men, in which and through whose unity alone the highest moral good can come to pass....[10]

This "union of such individuals" comprises an ethical common-wealth, which is a union of hearts, a kingdom of ends. This union is itself the togetherness in principle of all persons whose intentions and maxims accord with the moral law. In many respects, this union can be known to God alone, who only can know fully the true intentions of the heart. Thus there is only a quasi-visibility to the union of those holding a pure religious faith.

Supplementing this ideal union is the more practical union of those gathered under the rubrics of ecclesiastical faith, with its dependence not simply on pure reason but on revelations and dogmas built up over time. For all its flaws, the house of ecclesiastical faith nonethe-less provides a context within which pure religious faith might be exercised.

What is the ultimate end of evil? In Kant's earlier work, notably the *Critique of Practical Reason*, Kant's notion of God was developed as the source and destiny of the moral law. This element of a destiny beyond history was quite necessary, for justice requires that conform-ity to the moral law, which is the perfection of nature, should also result in the greatest happiness. Here Kant was not at all following a

eudaemonistic ethic wherein happiness becomes the sufficient reason
for moral conduct; instead, it was simply unthinkable for Kant that
the perfection of human nature should not be the most pleasing state:
virtue and happiness must coincide. As it happens, virtue and happiness do not coincide to any noticeable degree within earthly life. If
God is the guarantor that virtue is of infinite dimensions, God is also
the guarantor that justice—the coincidence of virtue and happiness
—will finally reign. Kant therefore argued that God is the source of
the moral law, the administrator of the moral law, and the eventual
judge of human obedience to the moral law in a future immortal state.

In his later *Religion within the Limits of Reason Alone*, immortality is
far more tenuous as the final answer to evil. In his first preface and a
very few passages within the body of the work, Kant refers somewhat
obliquely to a final end of immortality, guaranteed by God, where the
true union of hearts is finally achieved. However, the focus of his
solution to the problem of evil lies within the individual will as it
grasps the moral law with good intentions, and in society insofar as
there are any approximations of an ethical commonwealth. Evil
originates in human society, and finds its end in human society. The
protology of Adam and the eschatology of immortality function
symbolically to highlight the fundamental problem of evil and its
overcoming within history.

Through Kant, then, our contemporary age has received a powerful formulation of the problem of evil rooted in a corrupt will and
overcome by implications of an empowering divine action. The
analogies with Augustine's classical understanding of the turned will
are surely present, despite the profound differences. In classical
thought there is an emphasis upon an original purity from which the
will has turned. Kant's depiction of moral failure has rested on no
existential perfection achieved and lost. He uses the Adamic story
not as the symbol of a lost past but as a symbolic portrayal of our own
failures. The moral law exists as an archetypal goal impelling persons
toward achievement of the goal of universal moral rectitude. Thus
redemption cannot at all be a turning of the will back to an original
direction; it must be a novel overcoming of an existential and historical misdirection.

If Kant gave a modern expression of Augustine's emphasis on the
evil will, his near contemporary, Friedrich Schleiermacher, repeated
themes more clearly continuous with the emphasis upon finitude
given in Leibniz. Schleiermacher bypassed Kant's separation of evil

and the world of nature, and developed an understanding based not only upon finitude but upon the emerging notions of a developing, evolving world. Kant spoke of the capacity for the moral law as something imposed upon nature, and, therefore, as discontinuous with the natural world; Schleiermacher saw his version of our spiritual being, the God-consciousness, as emerging from our sensuous and rational nature in a continuous development which leads to our completion, and through us, to the completion of the world. This God-consciousness relates to the evolution of the world, to evil, and to redemption. In these respects, the awareness of the interdependence of all finite beings in an antithesis of dependence and freedom is of primary importance in the God-consciousness. Ultimately, this awareness of interdependence is itself dependent upon the overcoming of the finite antithesis in the feeling of absolute dependence. Following the discussion of interdependence, therefore, we will explore its relation to the feeling of absolute dependence.

Schleiermacher has a teleological view of the world's development, wherein the thrust toward the God-consciousness is the driving force in the creative evolution of the world.[11] In the prespiritual, sensuous beginnings of existence, there is an unconscious interdependence among the beings in the world; as existence develops toward consciousness, it does so toward the end that this interdependence, and the further absolute dependence of all finite beings upon God, will become recognized. Once recognized, this state of dependence is to become the criterion for conscious action.

Since the world is pushing toward such a state, the world as such is good—the sensuous nature alone is not evil. But the transition from such a state of primordial innocence in the world to one of evil, sin, and guilt lies in the change which spirituality brings about in existence. The position of a spiritual creature in the whole of nature is first that of an integral part of the whole; and second, it is that part of creation which, through knowledge, is to bind that creation into a meaningful as well as factual system of interrelationships. The creation is to receive a coherence and cohesiveness with the advent of human spirituality, through which the creation overcomes fragmentation, and is unified through recognized interdependence and mutual absolute dependence.

Obviously, then, this God-consciousness is to determine the attitude toward the world, but in doing so it requires a responsiveness which is obtained in the prespiritual condition. The prespiritual responsiveness centers primarily on the preservation of the responding organism, either as an individual or as a species. In such a case, the interrelatedness of the aspects of the world are irrelevant to the participants in the world, save as this interrelatedness is unconsciously utilized for the preservation of each being. Absolute dependence may be a fact of existence, but it is not yet a feeling, not a determining element of conscious existence.

The emergence of a spiritual being is completely antithetical to this situation; for, instead of requiring a concentration on the interests of one physical organism, spiritual being requires a reversal of perspective in which a new dimension emerges in the constitution of a being. In the prespiritual form of existence, survival of the organic unity is a sufficient determiner of action and/or being; but in the spiritual form, a self emerges which is only developed by its conscious relationship to all being in an expansiveness which "must include all others in itself."[12] This consciousness becomes the basis of its active being.

The resistance of the sensuous nature to the spirit is located just here in this reversal of what it is that constitutes the welfare of being. The self-centeredness which was natural and proper in the prespiritual sphere has given rise to a center of consciousness, but now a continuation in self-centeredness works against the best interests of that consciousness. Thus the limitations that Schleiermacher saw imposed upon the animal nature do not have that aura of arbitrariness, as in Kant, but are limitations that emerge from that lower nature in order to bring it and the whole creation to a higher state.

The problem in sin, then, is not only—nor, indeed, chiefly—that the senuous nature is ahead of the spiritual by virtue of its precedence in time,[13] but that the spiritual nature to which the sensuous has given rise must now transcend the sensuous inclinations toward exclusive and self-centered existence in favor of an inclusive and outward directed intention. The complicating factor is that this new mode of being must take place not in a radical break with the sensuous nature but in a continuity which simply directs one's sensuous nature toward the requirements of this new end. The emergence of the spiritual signifies that selfhood must break the bonds of a now false exclusiveness. Without spiritual consciousness, self-centeredness is proper; with spirituality, the actual interrelatedness of all things demands a response to the world which is a willing participation in the giving and receiving within the world which transcends the individual. Without spirituality, there is no evil, no sin, no guilt; with spirituality, there is immediate involvement in all three.

It can easily be seen that in this understanding of an emerging consciousness, "evil and sin are rooted in the temporal frame and the spatial individualization of existence,"[14] in which case the root of evil is finitude, but that nevertheless, "all evil is to be regarded as the punishment of sin, but only social evil as directly such, and natural evil as only indirectly."[15] Evil is now whatever obstructs the effectiveness of the God-consciousness, so that evil, while rooted in finitude, is still dependent upon the reaction to that finite obstructive situation. Because of God-consciousness, we are obligated to subsume the potentially destructive situation into conformity with the God-consciousness. Insofar as we succeed, evil never materializes; but insofar as we fail, our failure—by definition—actualizes the obstructiveness of the situation. Evil is relative to our ability to wield our God-consciousness in relationship to the world. Within this understanding there is no sense in which nature becomes fallen from a former perfection due to human sin; rather, nature as well as humanity is simply hindered in its press toward completion through the God-consciousness. Schleiermacher has performed the admirable feat of treating evil as rooted in finitude rather than solely in human freedom, and yet establishing that evil is human responsibility despite the finitude, since it comes about in our failure towards ourselves and the world.

How does an overcoming of evil fit this understanding? Schleiermacher portrays the Redeemer as the culmination and completion of creation, but this occurs in a curiously twofold sense, both from within the creation and from without. In Christ, there is a different union of creation and creator than that which follows normally from God's constant creativity in the world. Christ's person is both an emergence from nature, by which there is a continuity between Jesus and the creation, and a direct infusion by God of the consciousness of the interrelatedness of all being, with this consciousness being of such a strength that it is a sufficient determiner of all Christ's actions. The necessity of such a being is the final inability of creation to attain its own completion. It is as if God had been working through creation, propelling it toward that culmination of development which is the creation's becoming conscious of itself and God in spirituality, but that the creation cannot itself make the transition from fragmentation in the individual centeredness of its parts to the wholeness which is the gift of spiritual consciousness. Its resistance comes not in its sensuousness but at the very point of a God-consciousness which nevertheless continues in the dominance of the sensuous mode of being. The awareness of interdependence and absolute dependence is achieved, but the conformity of action with this awareness wavers in a hiatus created by habit, proceeding only feebly and partially to the fulfillment of the destiny which claims it. In Christ, then, who himself has been born through the route of humanity, God acts not only indirectly from within the creation but now directly upon creation. Christ becomes the bestowal upon humanity of that fullness of God-consciousness toward which the creation had been straining. Consequently, Christ is both the completion and the correction of creation; particularly, of course, at the point of difficulty, humanity. In Christ, creation is perfected, and the magnetism of this perfection draws all creation into a participation in this perfection which is now its own by virtue of Christ's humanity. His perfection, achieved within an interrelated system of nature, reverberates to the benefit of every participant in that system.[16]

Thus far we have centered on the aspect of the God-consciousness which relates to the interdependence within creation in the antithesis of dependence and freedom. Underlying this interdependence, and making its recognition possible, is what Schleiermacher refers to as the feeling of absolute dependence. This indicates an overcoming of the finite antithesis through positing an infinite antithesis of absolute dependence over against absolute freedom. "Everything depends upon God, but he himself upon nothing."[17]

There is no sense in which the creation exerts any counter-influence upon God. It is precisely this which constitutes the dependence as absolute.[18] The awareness of this absolute dependence undergirding all of finite being serves to encompass all the continuous variations of receptive activity within creation into one bond of unified dependence upon God. While the finite antithesis develops the "whatness" of each finite being, the infinite portion of the antithesis of dependence/freedom which falls to the creation is the foundation of the "whatness," the "whence" of its being.[19] This common dependence is the basis of union whereby the fragmentation of unrecognized interdependence is overcome. Schleiermacher feels only such a union can overcome the finite antithesis and bring the world to a conscious wholeness. Therefore, it is crucial to him that the world exerts no counterinfluence upon God; if it did, then the infinite antithesis which is to overcome the finite would itself devolve into the finite situation of mutual conditioning, and the basis for union would be lost.

If Kant reflects aspects of the Augustinian understanding of evil in the primacy of the turned will, Schleiermacher's affinities with Augustine are more centrally located in Augustine's notion of evil as privation of the good. Augustine viewed humanity as a mixture of being with nonbeing, and thus short of that mark of full actuality which in classical thought was necessary for complete being. This very lack of being required that the creature be sustained through clinging to Being in God. Otherwise, the creature suffered the threat of extinction and evil. Hence privation of being marked the possibility of the evil which was actualized in the turning will.

At just this point there is an amazing difference between Schleiermacher and Augustine. For Augustine, incompletion is a threat, the possibility of dissolution. But for Schleiermacher, incompletion is not negative; rather, it is a positive affirmation of one's participation in creativity. The incompletion of humanity and all of creation is the opportunity for humanity, giving the possibility for the creature's own creative contribution to the world. We can take this further and say that the world's incompletion becomes the means for the world's self-creativity. A true self-creativity becomes a radical thing now, and not quite like the freedom of classical thought. Whereas there freedom was the opportunity to maintain an already given nature, here incompletion and self-creativity provide the means to bring a nature into being. Far from having the negative overtones of privation, incompletion becomes the possibility for delight and an ever-newness to arise continually within creative finite existence. There is yet another distinction, for privation of being can look only to an essential past for humanity—one, it is hoped, to be regained— whereas incompletion looks to a novel future.

But note this: If incompletion becomes the source of evil, then we have moved beyond finitude itself to the possibilities of finitude. We no longer have the situation where finitude per se is evil, either explicitly or implicitly. In this important sense, Schleiermacher's use of finitude is an advance over both classical thought and the finitude given by Leibniz. While Leibniz, too, dwells on the possibilities of finitude, he relates these to a preestablished harmony which finally fulfills a function not unlike the givenness of essence in classical thought. Thus there is not the openness of finitude which Schleiermacher achieves. The possibilities are only secondarily enacted by the creature in creative interaction with the world; the ultimate source of selectivity with regard to possibilities lies in the infinite will of God. Therefore, the actualized Leibnitian possibilities are predetermined by final causation, and are simply part of the givenness of finitude. Schleiermacher achieves a notion of an incomplete world striving toward its unified wholeness, giving an intuition of an openness to creation. This openness toward the future is required for any genuine freedom of self-creativity. It is this perspective on finitude which avoids the necessity of equating finitude with evil.

A further implication follows. If incompletion and self-creativity push us toward the possibilities of finitude as a way of understanding evil, are possibilities then evil? The answer must be no. The possibilities of finitude are themselves neutral with regard to a valuation of good or evil, since in a context of incompletion, the valuation is relative to an actualized situation. It is not simply the incompletion of one finite being which is under consideration. Rather, the context is the world, a community of interrelated beings. But possibilities are abstract, relating to everything and to nothing: they cannot be "good" or "evil" in themselves. Only insofar as a concrete situation develops and, therefore, provides a definite context of actuality can a possibility be evaluated.

Even then, the evaluation of possibilities is absolutely limited; it becomes a judgment upon a possibility *as if* it were to be actualized in a specific situation. Possibilities do not submit to evaluation until they are presented to the imagination as actualizable, and then the value judgment upon that possibility is projected in terms of its future actuality. The possibility in itself is neutral; the context of actuality is required for the evaluation of possibility. The possibility is judged in terms of its function if and when it is actualized. This function, which is determinative of value, is finally relative to the totality of the context which would apply to the actualization. A complex matrix of interrelated events is the setting for actualization, and, therefore, for an evaluation. Insofar as no set of events is completely like another, each set provides a relatively novel context for evaluation. Any judgment of "good" or "evil" upon any possibility, therefore, requires first the context of actuality. Possibilities beyond any such context are simply that; sheer possibilities, neutral with regard to value.

In these two theories of a root understanding of evil derived from Kant and Schleiermacher, we see a contemporary bias toward an openness of creativity for the world. Once a preestablished essence which prescribes what existence will be in its every detail recedes to the background of thought, then the idea of self-creativity, and with it a notion of strong responsibility for the exercise of creativity, begin to qualify the notion of finitude. This is particularly apparent in Schleiermacher; it is present also in Kant insofar as the archetypal essence is a call to achievement of historical good. The twentieth century has inherited its own interpretation of evil from both of these men, but hardly from them alone.

The optimism which is present in both systems, manifest in Schleiermacher's confidence in Christ's completion of creation for all the earth, and Kant's awe at the presence and power of the archetypal moral law, will culminate in the optimistic development of Hegel. Hegel, viewed in his own time as the culmination of all systems, became a catalyst for yet more alternative systems. Ludwig Feuerbach's development of God as the projection of human consciousness, Karl Marx's extension of the dialectic of history into a mandate for social change, and Soren Kierkegaard's negation of the system in the face of the surdity of existence, are but three of the directions which evolved in reaction to the mighty Hegelian system. Friedrich Nietzsche is yet a fourth, with some kinship to the developments in Kierkegaard, but with his own insight into the plight of humanity when all things are no longer self-evidently rational, and there is no transcendental source of redemption from the evil of meaninglessness and fragmentation. Our next investigations will be into the question of evil, redemption, and God developed in Hegel and Nietzsche.

III

Hegel and Nietzsche:
Alienation and Meaninglessness

Both Kant and Schleiermacher wrote at the beginning of the nineteenth century. As pivotal figures, relating to both the past and the future, their analyses of evil are pertinent and pervasive in our time; but a more radical understanding of evil as alienation has taken its place beside them. Its roots are in Hegel, where alienation, or estrangement, was developed as a necessary moment in a process which culminated in reconciliation. Its more pessimistic development occurred in Friedrich Nietzsche.

Alienation was not considered an evil by Hegel himself. To the contrary, alienation, or estrangement, was an essential means to the realization of the fully self-conscious spirit. This, in turn, was the ground and reality of freedom, and issued into the highest form of human life, the community, or state. Yet the very genius and complexity of Hegel's system generated further systems, where the concept of alienation would take on meaning not necessarily intended by Hegel.

Within the root of Hegelian thought, finitude is the context where evil necessarily occurs, and where it is overcome through integral relation to the infinite. Perhaps this is best explicated by Hegel's parallel between the dynamics of self-conscious existence and historical existence. Self-consciousness is an achievement which occurs through three essential phases, with immediacy, or givenness, being the first phase. This mode of existence is immersed in the sheer physicality of existence, responding to its inner drives and outward circumstances. Thought most certainly may occur, but it is not yet *self*-conscious thought; it is simply a responsive consciousness. Hegel refers to such consciousness as the "natural" human being, describing it as follows:

> The first condition is an immediately natural state of the general appetites, desires, and tendencies. But this natural condition is one of consciousness. The consciousness of appetite is not without will. . . . Willing what is natural is, more precisely defined, evil. It is the willing of separation, the positing of one's singularity against others. Hence opposition is contained within it—in an immediate sense, the opposition between one's singularity and universality.[1]

The second phase involves a different relation to external existence: it is more than simply a response to otherness; it is a response to other as *other*. The differentiation which thus occurs involves at its deepest level the recognition of distance between self and other; it is in some sense an estrangement. Otherness is acknowledged, whatever it may be, as being also *not* the self. Here self-consciousness begins to emerge, but it is not yet at home with itself, not yet fully *self*-conscious. It is more oriented toward differentiation, which carries overtones of fragmentation and alienation.

> In the first place, subjective consciousness is posited as it is. As Spirit on the one side, it takes its beginning from the state of immediacy and raises itself to pure thinking, to the infinite, to the knowledge of God. . . . This passing beyond his natural state, beyond his implicit being, is what first of all constitutes the disunion or estrangement of man; it is that which posits the estrangement.[2]

The third phase in the coming-to-be of self-conscious existence involves reconciliation. Here the knowledge of otherness moves beyond simple differentiation, mediating to the self a knowledge of the unifying bond of rationality which connects other to self, self to other, in an interdependence which finally is known to be the truth of existence. It is only in and through rationality that this happens: the other can be *known*, and the self has the means within thought to be that knower; both alike participate in rationality, hence in connectedness. Thus immediacy of the first phase, and the alienation of the second phase, mark the pathway to the full possession of the self in the third phase.

The second stage of the third sphere is the elevation of Spirit out of its natural will, out of evil, out of the desires of individuality. . . . This elevation consists generally in the fact that man comes to consciousness of the universal in and for itself, and indeed is conscious of it as *his* essence. Thus man comes to consciousness of *his* infinity as existing in and for itself.[3]

Since this self-consciousness is precisely a mediated knowledge, it involves an "at-homeness" in the world which is essentially freedom.[4] This freedom is in the first place subjective, as the gain of self-determination which is made possible through self-knowledge; and in the second place objective, as the foundation for ordered communal existence in the state.

The freedom involved in full self-consciousness is in deep contrast to the instinctiveness of the first phase; freedom *is* freedom because of the structure and order which it provides for existence in a fundamentally rational reality. To know the self as a participant in an interconnected society is to know the self as constituted by rationally governed structures. If Kant had an ethical commonwealth which was a "union of hearts" as a goal for human existence, and Schleiermacher had the community of faith, Hegel has the ideal of a state which models itself after the rationality of many interrelated free beings, governing their interactions toward the good of each and all. Both Hegel and Schleiermacher use the notion of the family as seed for the model of the larger society, but in Hegel it goes beyond a faith community to encompass the structured society as a whole.[5] Since the structure is rational, it is in conformity with existence per se, and hence functions to maximize and mediate the freedom available through self-conscious existence. Qualities evoked by self-conscious existence are trust, which is the radical affirmation of the good of the whole, and the twin qualities of forgiveness and compassion, which recognize the graciousness required for fully communal existence.

There are two interrelated modes of evil to be derived from such a system, both having to do with Hegel's definition of evil as "generally speaking to be in a way that one ought not to be."[6] Both have to do with a freezing of the process of self-consciousness at one of its moments rather than moving to its completion, which is reconciliation. One of these modes is not unlike Schleiermacher's description of evil as the sense-immersed self, refusing the call to spiritual existence. For Hegel, the "natural" person, living a life only of gratifying the senses, is a contradiction in terms. The very nature of what it is to be human is to transcend the senses through reason, to consider one's relationship to nature, and to posit one's own nature as "other." The refusal of this call is in fact the contradiction of one's true nature, and is therefore an estrangement from one's true good which does not even recognize the fact of its estrangement. Thus the unalleviated immersion in physical existence is an evil; it manifests itself in selfishness and greed, violating the freedom of spiritual existence, which is essentially communal.

The second mode of evil stops with the second step of consciousness, or the positing of otherness as otherness without going on to recognize the essential affinity between self and other. This is the "bad infinity," manifesting itself in its extreme mode by the attribution of absolute transcendence to the other, or a full-scale infinity in the "wholly otherness" of God. This becomes a divestment of spirit in the world, and the impoverishment of the finite.

The falseness of the view is its failure to recognize that in the very rational structure of the world there is a witness to its relation to Spirit. Finitude is its own witness to infinitude, and infinitude likewise is infinite only in relation to the finite. Evil lies in creating a separation between the two and refusing to recognize the necessary reciprocity of the terms. It manifests itself in other-worldliness, which likewise tends toward the devaluation of forms of human community. Thus in this mode of evil, as in the first, alienation results. By remaining trapped in the false projection of the infinite, the self fails to realize its true selfhood, which is in fact in connection with the infinite.

If one can extrapolate evil as alienation from Hegel's depiction of what it is to be self-conscious, it is also the case that one can perceive this alienation in history. In fact, one can perceive history as the very unfolding of the moments of consciousness on a grand scale: the movement toward self-consciousness is the teleology of history. As such, history itself is taken up into a much vaster story in which the world becomes seen as the projected "other" of Spirit, which will realize its own self-consciousness and freedom through the mediation of the world.

The movement of history is the dynamism of infinite Spirit, positing itself in otherness through creation. Spirit immanent in the concreteness of creation is alienated from itself, is other to itself. Its coming to expression in human history is the process of its own self-mediation through otherness. World history is the process of the Spirit's unfolding to itself, its becoming as Absolute Spirit: "Every act of Spirit is thus only a comprehending of itself, and so the aim of all true science is simply this: that Spirit knows itself in everything in heaven and on earth."[7] This is the teleology of history, and it achieves its end insofar as humanity knows itself to be fundamentally united with that which it had termed "infinite" in its own repetition of the process. Thus there is a convergence of human self-consciousness, and the Spirit's self-consciousness; the realization of the one is by definition the actualization of the other: "God is God only so far as he knows himself: his self-knowledge is, further, a self-consciousness in man and man's knowledge of God, which proceeds to man's self-knowledge in God."[8]

Historically, this self-realization of Spirit can be seen through the teleological development of the world religions. Hegel posits three phases in the historical development of religions: a first phase, which he calls natural religion and which roughly corresponds to the "immediacy" stage of consciousness; a second phase, called "the religion of spiritual individuality," which corresponds with the second stage of consciousness; and a third phase, which is Absolute Religion, or the union of the infinite and finite which finally comes to expression in Christianity.[9] This, of course, corresponds with the reconciliation of self-consciousness. Throughout, there is a natural progression of Spirit pushing toward its own expression through the stages of religion.

Incarnation is the principle which constitutes Christianity as the Absolute Religion, for incarnation posits Spirit in the world coming to self-consciousness in and through the world, and thus reconciled with itself as reciprocally finite and infinite. Insofar as the specific incarnation of God in Christ is concerned, it is the specific emptying of God into the otherness of finitude, the total going over into that which is other, even including death.[10] The totality of this otherness becomes the very dynamism of resurrection, of the mediated return of Spirit to itself. This of course, is the realization of absolute freedom —Spirit not simply in itself, as an unconscious immediacy, nor simply for itself, posited in otherness, but rather as the fullness of being both in and for itself, which is absolute freedom. The freedom follows from the givenness of all existence as the home of Spirit in the union of finite and infinite.

Even the freedom of Spirit, however, is no individualized autocracy, but is as necessarily communal as is human freedom. This follows from the rational or reasonable nature of freedom—it is an ordered reality, based upon recognition of the presence of the Spirit (or rationality) implicit and sometimes explicit within all existence. Freedom is therefore structured for the facilitation of the continuous realization of Spirit; it is a freedom of and within community. Thus the resurrection of Christ issues necessarily into a communal form of existence wherein the reconciliation of finite and infinite might be continuously achieved.[11] The freedom of Christ is manifest in the structure of a community.

However, only rational reflection upon that structure can bring its fullness to expression, and hence actualize the full reconciliation between finite and infinite. This is the task of philosophy, discovering the significance of the stories told by history. Thus we come full circle, for it is reason, realizing the rational structure of existence and the import of that rational structure, which is the realized goal of history. In this realization, freedom becomes absolute. Its natural manifestation is through creation of the all-encompassing State.

Thus in Hegel the structure of thought is the pattern and teleology of history. The goal is freedom, the union in thought of infinite and finite, universal and particular, ego and other. The absolute freedom of this union is the comprehension that the determinations of one's being are ultimately the determinations which are posited by one's own consciousness. Such is the ideal, the ultimate and realized aim of Absolute Spirit.

The convergence of the analysis of consciousness and the history of religions is matched as well by history as a whole. Here in particular we can see the historical form of the alienations encountered in the analysis of consciousness. However, the alienation in history may not be quite so amenable to the final reconciliation of finite and infinite as that obtained in a single individual's or society's existence.

Hegel's *Philosophy of History* follows the unfolding of Spirit in the history of the world. In this work, two elements are necessary in the thrust of the Spirit toward the goal of Absolute Freedom: the universal idea and the passions of the individual. The universal idea is analogous to unmediated Spirit; it is an undifferentiated unity which pushes toward realization of differentiation for the purpose of a fullness of self-knowledge. In history, this universal idea becomes differentiated as the urge toward conscious individuality manifesting itself in the infinite variety within the world.

In considering Hegel's development, we might posit that the second element, the passions, poses the ambiguity of fulfilling two opposing functions. On the one hand, we can see the passions as the instrument of the idea in its mode of conscious differentiation, humanity. Spirit truly becomes *other* precisely through the passionate rather than intentionally rational existence of human societies. Hence such existence is Spirit's second step on the road toward Absolute Spirit. But on the other hand, the passions are the instruments of humanity within its own first mode of immediate or natural existence. What is the second stage of consciousness for Spirit is the first stage of consciousness for humanity. At that first stage, the ends of humanity can in fact be quite contrary to the Spirit's continuing movement toward reconciliation. Thus the passions can be directed toward continuing differentiation insofar as humanity simply lives out of its own unreflective immediacy. This latter can be a block to the purposes of the former; it is the necessary risk that Spirit takes in otherness.

Hegel's treatment lends itself to the image of a mighty force, called Spirit, creating the world for the sake of its own self-realization through differentiation and reconciliation. But since the world was created for Spirit's *self*-realization, the imprint of the Spirit's self is indelibly in that world. That blind imprint has a power both derived and, by virtue of its created nature, separate: it pushes creation toward a great multitude of forms of differentiation.[12] Insofar as these forms of difference come to a consciousness of their mutual origin and identity with the Spirit which gave them birth, then they are a return to Spirit of what is now the fullness of Spirit's being, or its own transformation into the fully self-conscious Absolute Spirit. Through the world, the Spirit comes to itself, and through the Spirit, the world comes to itself. Both Spirit and World together in reciprocal self-consciousness constitute Absolute Spirit. The key term is reciprocity.

The movement of history which marks the progression of the universal aim comes about when the universality of Spirit erupts through the individuality of human societies, shaping passions beyond immediacy to the service of the future. The passions which make up that society become the means of universal advancement. The cost of the World Spirit's drive through history in its self-development is the very carnage of history wrought by the clash of individual and the universal passions. In moving paragraphs, Hegel speaks of the wreckage inherent in the process, of the "slaughterbench" character of history, wherein individual happiness is the victim of the progressive movement.[13] One description is given in Hegel's *Encyclopedia:*

Reason is as cunning as it it powerful. Cunning may be said to lie in the intermediative action which, while it permits the objects to follow their own bent and act upon one another till they waste away, and does not itself directly interfere in the process, is nevertheless only working out its own aims. With this explanation, Divine Providence may be said to stand to the world and its process in the capacity of absolute cunning. God lets men do as they please with their particular passions and interests; but the result is the accomplishement of—not their plans, but his, and these differ decidedly from the ends primarily sought by those whom he employs.[14]

The evil which emerges has the character of an unfortunate but necessary alienation. Within the moments of consciousness, alienation is a part of the process which produces reconciliation, and, therefore, alienation is taken up into the awareness of freedom. But if these moments are spread through history, the process is threatened with the equivalence of the "frozen" stages of alienation which do not go beyond themselves. How do those who represent the natural or the objective stages participate in the final stage of reconciliation, or Absolute Spirit? Are the "slaughterbench" victims redeemed?

The plight of history is that it necessitates individual and social existence in alienation and all its consequences. The particularity of finite existence is not in its deepest sense the true self of the world; the world *is* differentiated universal, but *exists* as the many particularities, driven by passions in most cases to emphasize particularity. As the point of consciousness in the world, humanity lives with an inherent contradiction of its nature. Caught between the undifferentiated universal and its eventual full realization as Spirit, humanity belongs to both, is necessary to both, and yet is alienated through the very necessity of particularity. Historically, the realization of the ultimate union of the differentiated within the universal is too long in coming for most people.[15] Alienation from one's nature, and suffering the works of alienation, mark the passionate existence of persons throughout the greater part of history. Paradoxically, this alienation is itself necessary for the ultimate union, since it is the impetus which moves the World Spirit toward that final union. The goal of history becomes the justification of history, but it is only a justification—a reconciliation—if all the moments of history participate in this reconciliation. Only insofar as the "wasted" moments have been taken up into Spirit as aspects of differentiation mediated back into the ultimate consciousness of Spirit is the ultimate purpose of history achieved.

In Hegel's initial development of the theme of alienation, the universal quality of that which finally overcomes alienation is essential to the fullness of reconciliation. His theodicy rests on the return to the Absolute Spirit of each element of particularity; that which has been estranged, whatever its time or place, is reunited to the universal from which it initially developed. All particularity has been the Spirit sporting with itself, and the mediation of that particularity back into the universal constitutes the realized self-knowledge of the universal, wherein it becomes Absolute Spirit.

Reconciliation can therefore be considered under two aspects: There can be the Spirit knowing itself, which is reconciliation with itself; and in complementary fashion, there can be the awareness in the particular of its true union with the universal. Reconciliation which follows an essential self-diremption of Spirit such as Hegel posits involves two merged forms of consciousness in reconciliation. Since Hegel holds that the final union does not negate the particular as if it had never been, but only negates the separation of the particular, he is bound to use both aspects of consciousness in Spirit. Spirit must contain the particular's own knowing subjectivity within the universal. Otherwise, if the vast waste from the slaughterbench of history is mediated into the universal unbeknownst to the myriad particulars so constituted, how is it in any sense a reconciliation which has benefitted from the estrangement? In such a case, the particular would be fully negated, not mediated; only insofar as the particular consciousness goes beyond the existential condition of estrangement does it become reconciled. Otherwise, the last condition of the universal does not differ significantly from the first. The full negation of the particular consciousness leads again to the undifferentiated identity of the universal. Thus reconciliation as developed in connection with existential estrangement requires not only a universal in the form of Spirit comprehending the moment of its past, but a universal which in some sense retains the consciousness of its various projected modes of objective/subjective particularity.

Hegel recognizes the need of such a reconciliation, and yet an ambiguity arises, for his system does or does not provide such a moment, depending on the extent of his crucial identification of the Absolute Spirit with humanity's own self-consciousness. If, as sometimes seems apparent, humanity's own consciousness exhausts the notion of the absolute, then reconciliation is a paltry achievement from an overall view—the elect are few indeed. If in fact the true reciprocity of Spirit and world holds, then a Hegelian analysis of evil as alienation is ultimately taken up into the transformation of reconciliation. The "left" and "right" wing Hegelians witnessed to the ambiguity, and to the varying interpretations of the necessity of "God" in the Hegelian system. It is the left-wing school which primarily concerns us here, as we continue to explore the formulations of evil which depend upon an understanding of finitude necessitating evil.

The subsequent perception of evil as alienation broke away from Hegel's formulations but not from his formula. The concept of humanity existing in an historical alienation from that which must be attained was developed by Marx, Feuerbach, Schopenhauer, Nietzsche, Sartre, and eventually the liberation theologians of our own time. Each of them retains, though in variously altered fashion, the Hegelian principle that human nature must find relation to that which is beyond itself, and yet to which it essentially belongs. Only in such union can one overcome historical alienation. Whether this ultimacy be conceived as social and economic justice, or as ideal projections, or the driving force of the universe, or as being-in-itself in opposition to the necessarily negating force of consciousness, it is a principle which demands unification with itself and yet, paradoxically, against itself. Human existence is a predicament, tinged with an element of tragedy according to how possible that needed union is. Insofar as the alienation is considered evil, evil is the inescapable context of existence; but insofar as the ultimate principle has a belongingness to the human condition, then one's condition retains responsibility within the evil circumstances of existence. Such responsibility becomes defined by the degree to which conduct tends to intensify or alleviate the condition of alienation.

If the element which provides reconciliation is taken out of a genuinely universal sphere, so that it in no sense transcends history but is instead totally immanent within it, the evil of history is finalized, and alienation is the dominant characteristic of existence for all but those who ride the crest of history's wave at the point where reconciliation is made possible. Alienation as evil in that case retains its dominion over the vast majority of humankind. Yet even for the select few who attain reconciliation, a new dimension to evil begins to emerge from this totality of immanence. When there is nothing beyond historical existence in the world, then there exists no external measure for humankind, and no aim beyond humanity itself.

Though one may posit an aim for oneself, that aim has no meaning beyond the self, so that with the death of the self there is also a death of meaning.

This implication of Hegelian thought is clearly seen by Friedrich Nietzsche, who proclaimed himself the prophet of nihilism as a result. He typically states the dilemma in the conciseness of an aphorism: "The aim is lacking; 'why?' finds no answer."[16] The journeying of the alienated one becomes not a purposeful stride toward a clearly defined goal, but suddenly a faltering step in the desert of futility. The ultimate principle which could overcome alienation and unite one with one's destiny becomes a mirage offering no water for one's thirst, so that now even alienation becomes an illusion: there is nothing from which one could be alienated. Nietzsche saw even this loss of an illusion strangely taking the place of the illusion, perpetuating the same mistaken struggle for a dimension beyond the world which simply is not there.

Kant had begun with human consciousness in terms of the a priori moral law within it; Schleiermacher analyzed consciousness in terms of absolute dependence; Hegel had seen it as incorporating an aim worked out in history; Nietzsche attacked all three. Insofar as each of the three had provided a foundation for morals, Nietzsche's attack undermined each basis, but his purpose was far from simply nihilism as an end in itself. Instead, Nietzche intended to hasten the full advent of the dawning nihilism in order that it might be overcome in a transvaluation of values. In the process Nietzsche gave profound expression to the meaninglessness which threatens human existence in the loss of transcendence.

Just as Hegel did not consider alienation to be the root of evil, neither did Nietzsche consider meaninglessness to be that root. Meaninglessness was rather symptomatic of "the last man," of the end of a culture which had been based on an empty transcendence as its measure. Evil in Nietzsche's estimation was rooted in *ressentiment*, which is the perversion of that basic instinct through which Nietzsche defined life, the will to power. When people find themselves unable to project the will to power in a sphere of influence beyond themselves, they tend to turn it inward in what becomes a self-inflicted weakness, whose expression then becomes a morality which is designed to justify the weakness. Nietzsche desired the overcoming of this falseness in the transvaluation of values, the movement beyond *ressentiment* into an acceptance of life lived to its creative fullness, in the knowledge that the life one creates for oneself is all one has.

In the process of describing this falseness which must be overcome, Nietzsche spoke first of the evidence of this falsity becoming open to our experience. He saw *ressentiment* as having issued into a culture of transcendence, whereby the world is judged ultimately by that which is beyond itself, so that the world is "real" only in relation to that which is beyond it. But the events of the nineteenth century had, in Nietzsche's estimation, brought that transcendent reality into question.[17] With that reality crumbling into an illusion, the contingent reality and value of the world collapses as well. Nihilism—metaphysical in the loss of transcendence, and axiological in the loss of the transcendently based values[18]—descends upon the world. The realization of this loss is slow; its magnitude numbs the senses to its presence, so that it is denied at first in a blind and clumsy resistance. This, Nietzsche held, was the condition of his own day, but the full knowledge of the loss was inevitable in a time to come—our time. In *The Gay Science*, the prophet of the loss is a madman, for the light of a transcendently based reason has gone out, though the blind do not perceive it.[19] Yet the perception must dawn, and with it, the full experience of nihilism.

Nietzsche, referring to the metaphysical nihilism of the loss of transcendence, related the problem to the loss of all aim or goal in history. Scheiermacher had spoken of a creation moving toward a completion, and visualized this completion in the Redeemer; Hegel had understood all history as the teleological realization of Absolute Spirit; others, in the increasingly evolution-conscious age, had likewise spoken of purpose and fulfillment in history; but to Nietzsche, insofar as these goals lay beyond the world, receiving their validity through their transcendent dimensions, the goals must inevitably be revealed to be illusory. His greatest discussion of nihilism occurs in *The Will to power*, particularly in fragment 12 (A):

And now one realizes that becoming aims at nothing and achieves nothing. —Thus disappointment regarding an alleged aim, or, universalized, the realization that all previous hypotheses about aims that concern the whole "evolution" are inadequate (man no longer the collaborator, let alone the center, of becoming).

Some sort of unity, some form of "monism": this faith suffices to give man a deep feeling of standing in the context of, and being dependent on, some whole that is infinitely superior to him, and he sees himself as a mode of the deity. —"The well-being of the universal demands the devotion of the individual"—but behold, there is no such universal! At bottom, man has lost the faith in his own value when no infinitely valuable whole works through him; i.e., he conceived such a whole in order to be able to believe in his own value.

But as soon as man finds out how that world is fabricated solely from psychological needs, and how he has absolutely no right to it, the last form of nihilism comes into being: it includes disbelief in any metaphysical world and forbids itself any belief in a *true* world.

What has happened, at bottom? The feeling of valuelessness was reached with the realization that the overall character of existence may not be interpreted by means of the concept of "aim," the concept of "unity," or the concept of "truth."[20]

Aim, unity, and truth, conceived as a relationship to that which was beyond the world, sufficed to give meaning to the world. But the aim, the unity, and the truth are creations of humans as the ultimate expressions of a rationally developed *ressentiment*; as such, they are psychologically based, and not ontologically based. They prove illusory, and the loss of the illusion means the loss of the values and meaning associated with the illusion. Insofar as we cannot dissociate value and meaning from transcendence, there is inevitably nihilism. Humanity, frantic for its meaning, is then pictured by Nietzsche as substituting one illusion for another, and finally, in the lowest degradation of all, pinning "meaning" on the very loss of the illusion. In this case, "there is no aim, unity, or truth" becomes itself the aim, the unity, and the truth in a positing of nihilism as the meaning of the world. "Rather than want nothing," writes Nietzsche in *On the Genealogy of Morals*, "man even wants nothingness."[21]

But Nietzsche himself intended a transcendence of nihilism—it is an age which must come as the undoing of the former falsity, but once tasted, it is to be transcended. Nietzsche himself epitomized this movement.

That I have hitherto been a thorough-going nihilist, I have admitted to myself only recently: the energy and radicalism with which I advanced as a nihilist deceived me about this basic fact. When one moves toward a goal it seems impossible that "goallessness as such" is the principle of our faith.

It is only a question of strength: to have all the morbid traits of the century, but to balance them through a superabundant, recuperative strength. The strong man.

To explore the whole sphere of the modern soul, to have sat in its every nook—my ambition, my torture, and my happiness.

Really to *overcome* pessimism—a Goethean eye full of love and good will as the result.[24]

The *"Übermensch,"* the affirmer of this world, the conscious creator and projector of values: this to Nietzsche is the overcoming of nihilism, and the stage of humanity which is now possible, given the dissolution of the former transcendence. The *Übermensch* is possible as the afterword of nihilism; for this reason, Nietzsche intended a full disclosure of the nihilism, hastening the full advent of its arrival, precisely in order that its overcoming might also arrive. He understood the modern consciousness to have reached a final plateau which has revealed the misdirection of the whole human program insofar as it has considered itself in terms of something beyond itself. Nietzsche must expose this, showing its barrenness, and then point the way to what he understood as the only reconstruction possible: the preparation for a new kind of person, beyond good and evil as it had been formerly understood. But first the nihilism which was the fruit of the former way must be tasted to the full, and then the new species could emerge—not through evolution, but through the affirmation of life as it is given and forged in our creative interaction with the world. The ultimate signification of this affirmation of life is given in Nietzsche's culminating doctrine, the notion of the eternal recurrence of all things.

Since the nihilism of a dissolution of transcendence has indeed characterized much of our own time, and since it has also, as Nietzsche prophesied, contributed a sense of meaninglessness and absurdity to our perception of evil, we must give particular attention to Nietzsche's understanding of the overcoming of this evil. There is a deep problem in his resolution which, if it is so, does not answer nihilism, but simply increases it. In this case, Nietzsche's "remedy" becomes a part of the illness which must still be taken up into the contemporary understanding of evil, requiring an answer in any comprehensive formulation of the overcoming of evil which is sufficient for us.

For Nietzsche, the answer to nihilism comes in its greatest strength when the will to power demonstrates itself in a "yes" to life to the degree that one could will again that the entirety of one's life—and all of history as well—should recur endlessly, like the eternal turning of a cosmic wheel. Such an affirmation is of all things the hardest. It requires that one will not only the joys but the suffering, the brutalities, the pettiness, the tragedies—everything which has hitherto impelled humanity to seek a transcendence which overcomes the finite condition must now be accepted, affirmed, and willed to recur eternally in precisely the same way as it has been experienced.

In *Thus Spake Zarathustra*, where Nietzsche most fully develops this theme, Parts III and IV are concerned with the temptations away from such an affirmation.[25] The nausea at the thought of the inanities and failures and sufferings happening again, and again, and again; the pity for humanity which demands, when a betterment is impossible, at least a conclusion to human misery—the depth of such considerations cries out against the doctrine of eternal recurrence. Yet to deny the "yes" to the doctrine on such a basis is also to deny the ultimate affirmation of life, this life. To take the suffering and pettiness into oneself and affirm them in recurrence is the ultimate step in overcoming weakness: it is the supremacy of Nietzsche's *amor fati*, and the triumphant exercise of the will to power.

The symbolic power of eternal recurrence is undeniably great, conveying as it does the total impact of Nietzsche's philosophy. However, there is a puzzle within the doctrine, for if there is an eternal recurrence, then everything "happens" only once. There can be no novelty whatsoever in recurrence, in which case there can be no "again-ness" involved. The doctrine understood literally requires that there be no "second, third, . . . nth" time of happening.[26] Since there is no cumulative effect in the cycles, the "onceness" of this time is repeated every time, and repetition adds nothing. The force of eternal recurrence, then, has no meaning beyond that which it obtains in the consciousness of the one affirming the doctrine.

And yet the doctrine is redemptive. "To redeem what is past, and to transform every 'It was' into 'Thus would I have it!'—that only do I call redemption!" speaks Zarathustra.[27] The very affirmation of the past gives that past a retroactive meaning for the yea-sayer. In willing that very past, it is accepted into the self, giving it the meaning of the yea-sayer's own affirmative creativity. The meaning of the present is projected onto the past, so that through the yea-sayer of the present, the past receives a meaning from beyond itself. The affirmation of the past in the "thus I willed it" is the attribution of worth, meaning, redemption to that past. This much follows from the symbolic power of the myth of eternal recurrence.

There is a second mode of redemption if the myth be considered literally, as Nietzsche appears to have thought. In an eternal recurrence, the past would be continuously preserved; nothing of the past could be lost. The affirmations of insignificant people, even the despised "herd," are affirmed again throughout each infinite repetition of the same events. One's meaning does not die with death, however paltry that meaning has been. One's meaning merely awaits the time of its "resurrection," its moment of eternal repetition. However, this dimension of meaning and value is realized only in the consciousness of the mythic one Nietszche called the "*Übermensch*"; it is a value which transcends the actual living of each event in history.

But the *Übermensch* has not yet come. She[28] awaits the fulfillment of the nihilistic vision—she is the dawn which follows the nihilistic night of despair. Nietzsche foreshadows *Übermensch* in his heralding of this approaching new age, but this race of yea-sayers belongs yet to the future.

This *Übermensch*, then, who is symbolized through the affirmation of eternal recurrence, does she not function as that which gives meaning to all human beings? Does she not provide an explanation of history's significance, and the redemption of history's sorrows? As such, does she not constitute a new aim for history, a new transcendence by which to give value to all humanity through an overarching perspective on the past? The very mode by which the *Übermensch* will arrive is a transcendence of the world, for she is not an evolutionary, emergent development—as if she were some sort of "next stage" on the scene of an evolving world. On the contrary, she transcends such developmental being through the very will by which she comes into being. She turns upon history through an act of sheer will. It is not that she affirms history because she must, as a natural and organic product of history; she affirms history solely because she thus wills the affirmation. As such, the *Übermensch* is contingent upon her own will for her being, and through this act of will she transcends the entire process of history. Through such willful, "this-worldly" transcendence, history is redeemed.

Is it? Is not this transcendence, too, an "illusion" since it belongs finally, only to the consciousness of a few? Is redemption, after all, the province of so small a group? If so—and it must be, since eternal recurrence is not felt as a factor beyond such transcendent ones—then Nietzsche's prescription for overcoming the evil of nihilism must lead to despair for the many. It depends upon the transcendence of a consciousness which is itself tied to the fleetingness of time, and whose affirmations are finally only applicable to that one consciousness. Knowing this, there must be the recognition that the redemption of history through the *Übermensch* in and for itself is as nothing, for the very affirmation which is thus given to history dies with the *Übermensch*. Given this finite transcendence, the past does not participate in its effect, and even the pseudo-redemption which is involved in the affirmation of the *Übermensch* pays the toll of time in death.

Nietzsche has already phrased the problem: "How should a tool be able to criticize itself when it can use only itself for the critique? It cannot even define itself."[29] When the individual is the measure of self worth, how is there any measure at all? Upon what basis, and for what reason, is the measure called one thing and not another? Is the "yea-saying" involved in eternal recurrence any more authentic a way of being than some other mode one may choose? What does it finally matter? If there is no measure beyond human existence, there is no meaning beyond human existence; the transcendence devised through affirmation suffers the same fate as the transcendence based on an illusion. The meaning given by the *Übermensch* becomes as transient as the *Übermensch*, and the ultimacy which redeemed that one is "ultimate" relative only to that one.

When Nietzsche proclaimed our aloneness in the universe, and the need for self-affirmation, he could use only nihilism, meaninglessness, and aimlessness to characterize our tendency to look beyond ourselves for some reason for being. Meaninglessness was the evil with which one had to wrestle in the slowly dawning comprehension of the "death of God." The tragedy which threatens even Nietzsche's joyous affirmation of human self-creativity in a universe where there is only that is the fact that meaninglessness pervades this realm, too. There is no ultimate overcoming of the problem of meaning when there is nothing which is ultimate beyond the human sphere—joyous affirmation, tragedy, or absurdity are equal options in the ephemerality of one's evaluation of one's own values. Not even eternal recurrence can inject meaning into the values, since the recurrence does not even add the value of repetitiveness; it has neither value not existence beyond the consciousness of the affirmer. The legacy of Nietzsche for our understanding of evil is, then, simply the meaninglessness which he prophesied. Whether we take his profound analysis of nihilism or his positive construction of the *Übermensch*, nothingness enshrouds the transitory world.

Kant, Schleiermacher, Hegel, and Nietzsche have given us powerful expressions of our contemporary experience of evil—a will which betrays us through a denial of a nature we feel ought to be, an incompletion of being which strives toward a comprehensiveness of being which ever eludes us, an alienation which depends upon some form of transcendence for its overcoming, and the threat of meaninglessness, aimlessness, aloneness, haunting even the most vibrant affirmation of a value which is doomed to perish.

The very "evilness" of the evil will, incompletion, alienation, and meaninglessness lies in the sense of wrongness. To name such things negatively implies a better condition that calls us, that belongs to us, but which evades us. We are alienated from the implied good, to whatever degree. But the "good" is, in this lack of transcendence, as various as the evils. There is no unified or well-defined sense of good or evil, and our perception yields a bits and pieces world of fragmentation.

We began our discussion by locating two fundamental modes of understanding the cause of evil in the world, freedom and finitude. Augustine developed the long dominant tradition of evil rooted in misused freedom, and Leibniz gave recognition, wittingly or no, to the shift to the problem of finitude. In the four philosophers considered in these two chapters, finitude likewise has the dominance as the reason for evil. Even Kant, who most closely approximates the Augustinian view, finally implies an inevitability to the evil of the will within the conditions of finitude. We also see in these four a progression with regard to the resolution of evil. For Kant, however ambiguously, it still includes a realm of immortality, as well as an ethical commonwealth in history. For Schleiermacher the emphasis is upon a completion in history, already realized in the Redeemer. While there is a deep intimation that the union with the Redeemer must be eternal, there is no clear explication of this; the focus rests with histroy. Hegel's deeply complex cosmology speaks of a togetherness of infinitude and finitude, so that a Spirit which is more than this world is realized in and through this world; but it is ultimately unclear whether or not there is a participation of this world in the world of Spirit beyond human history. And for Nietzsche, of course, the answer is quite clear. Increasingly, then, insofar as an understanding of evil related fundamentally to finitude is divorced from eschatological resolution, history remain unredeemed as Hegel's slaughterbench.

In order to attempt a resolution, it is necessary to take the fragmented interpretations of evil compiled in these various systems of thought, and unify them within a single theory. This means tending to the pole of freedom as well as the pole of finitude, since its influence continues. The next step, then, is to pull these threads of evil together under the rubric of Whitehead's process thought. We must show how his conceptuality gives account to each of these dimensions of evil; only then can we use this philosophy to formulate the answering redemption, and to speak of the redemptive God.

IV

A Whiteheadian Theory of Evil

The understanding of evil which puts the locus of the problem upon the subjective pole of the human will continues to shape Christian experience today, but the dominance has shifted to the understanding which sees the inevitably competitive and evolutionary structure of the world as the fundamental reason for evil. While theologians may deal systematically from one basis or the other, most common experience is affected by both perceptions. Likewise, the various effects of evil, whether rooted in the will or in finitude, continue to be used to interpret and name the threats encountered in existence. This is true at the societal as well as the personal level, with the problem undoubtedly magnified in the late twentieth century by the enormity of social problems. Holocaust, apartheid, nuclear winter, environmental destruction, poverty, hunger, and the ever-pervasive threat of terrorism and war transcend national and cultural boundaries, tinging existence throughout the planet with anxiety.

Thus the evils named throughout our tradition continue to shape the contemporary interpretation of evil: the sin of a misdirected will that raises the finite to the infinite in idolatrous loves; the problem of an inevitable conflict in values; the perverse moral failure to act for the good of an ethical commonwealth; incompleteness of being; alienation from oneself, one's destiny, one's projected good, or one's true society; the meaninglessness which is entailed in the loss of a

61

sense of a unifying transcendence, and its corollary, fragmentation. Each and all add their edge to the way we name the plight of existence. Insofar as they can be unified into a single theory of evil, we will be empowered to express more adequately that which is required as a redemptive answer to the problem of evil, and to develop a coherent doctrine of the redemptive God in the process.

The challenge, of course, is to develop a theory which can embrace both poles adequately, and thus incorporate the various implications with consistency and coherence. The categories of Alfred North Whitehead's process philosophy provide a basis for developing such a unified theory, since the intrinsic relativity of these categories requires that everything be considered in subjective terms of its own dynamics of becoming, and in objective terms of the entire universe that conditions becoming and is in turn affected by it. "Freedom in community" is the fundamental structure allowing both subjective and objective poles of evil to be held in creative tension.

To develop the structure of freedom in community, we must examine Whitehead's own understanding of evil. One of his most succinct statements on the subject is found in *Adventures of Ideas*.[1]

The doctrine has been stated that the experience of destruction is in itself evil; in fact that it constitutes the meaning of evil. We find now that this enunciation is much too simple-minded. Qualifications have to be introduced, though they leave unshaken the fundamental position that 'destruction as a dominant fact in the experience' is the correct definition of evil.

The intermingling of Beauty and Evil arises from the conjoint operation of three metaphysical principles: (1) that all actualization is finite; (2) that finitude involves the exclusion of alternative possibility; (3) that mental functioning introduces into realization subjective forms conformal to relevant alternatives excluded from the completeness of physical realization (*AI* 259).

The three principles Whitehead names act conjointly, since they involve dynamics which are operative in every actuality. Actuality is definite, which is to say finite, through its selection of data from its past for inclusion in its own becoming in light of its own immediate future. However, each of the principles should be considered at some length individually to gain a deeper understanding of what Whitehead means by affirming that destruction is the definition of evil.

The experience of destruction which is named as evil involves the loss of possibility and the loss of actuality, and it is an inevitable consequence of finitude. Finitude itself carries several implications in this regard. First, there is an inescapable definiteness to actuality; it is precisely this and not that. By no means does this exclude deep complexity from the "thisness," such that many ambiguities of meaning might be involved. But all actuality has a stubborn facticity to it, which is why Whitehead then goes on to explicate the consequences of this facticity in terms of excluded alternatives.

Second, all finitude involves an ambiguous form of destruction which is both completion and perishing—an intermingling of Beauty and Evil. This follows from the structure of existence according to Whitehead's model of the actual entity, signifying the basic dynamics of all existent reality whatsoever. The actual entity is an instance of creativity, dynamically unifying its entire past into its own present. This unification actualizes some unique possibility for the entity, given its particular locus with respect to its past. With the attainment of its own creative ideal of unification, the entity is then subjectively complete, becoming influential in what the future can be. Just as the entity had to account for every element in its own past, becoming itself within the parameters thus defined, even so it now has provided parameters of interpretation and influence for its successors. In the process, creativity passes from the entity's own internal activity to external activity, or what Whitehead calls a movement from concrescence to transition. The entity becomes "objectively immortal," a stubborn fact for the future. Its immediacy has perished, causing Whitehead to echo Plato in describing the actual entity as that which becomes, but "never really is." This loss of immediacy is the primary meaning of evil as perpetual perishing in Whitehead. It is called "perpetual" perishing in that he conceives existence to be compiled by innumerable instances of creativity, or actual entities, each of which comes into being and perishes in rapid succession.[2]

An image to help grasp the sheer numbers involved might be that of a mighty waterfall, greater than Niagara or Victoria. If each drop of water which has ever fallen over the underlying ledges and cliffs for millenia of time could be conceived as an actual entity, reaching the edge and tumbling down, crashing into the waiting river which it itself helps to create, only to be succeeded on the ledges above by innumerable others, the force of "perpetual perishing" might be grasped. Each drop moves into the river, but the waterfall as a whole continues through time. Perpetual perishing is the loss of each drop of actuality, even though there is an endurance of the total effect.

Eventually that effect, too, passes, to be succeeded by that which new conditions make possible. Existence involves an inevitable loss of immediacy, a death, at microscopic and macroscopic levels.

The exclusion of alternative possibility is the second dimension of evil named by Whitehead. Its fundamental reference is to the decision of the entity with regard to its own becoming. This decision relates to past, present, and future, and is based on the need incumbent upon each entity to unify all of the forces affecting it from its past in a way which is congruent with its own development. Whitehead calls this the category of subjective harmony. He develops it by pointing to the reality that the past is made up of many things, each representing contrasting values, while the present entity is, of course, one. The many must be reduced to one determinate feeling.

In this context, the exclusion of alternative possibility relative to the past means that some concrete values must simply be negated as incompatible with the present. Since Whitehead terms the feeling by one entity of the value within another as "prehension," this means that some values previously achieved will be negatively prehended. The meaning of that negated past is lost insofar as it concerns the presently concrescing entity.

With regard to the present, there is more than one way to unify the past: by selecting one mode of determination, the others are consigned to nonbeing, and they are lost. On the macroscopic level of human existence, this is illustrated by the simple reality that to choose to do one thing inescapably involves choosing not to do something else; to choose to become this eliminates the possibility of becoming that: existence is a matter of choices, and choice is by definition exclusive. There is an exclusion of some value in the achievement of any value, and this can be felt as simple tension, as pleasure, or as evil, depending upon the context. Whether valued positively or negatively, it is loss.

With respect to the exclusion of alternative possibility relative to the future, this is primarily immediate, and involves—as stated above—the immediate choice of one's becoming. But there is a long-term implication as well, since the choice of one's immediate future carries within it an anticipation of various results of that choice beyond the present moment. Just as the present entity has eliminated some values in the past, even so the future may adversely value this present achievement. The perpetuation of meaning is dependent upon one's successors. When the future chooses to respond to one's values negatively, then to that degree one's own value is lost in the ongoing stream of existence.

This whole category of the exclusion of alternative possibility involves the use of negative prehensions. In Whitehead's system, negative prehensions are essential to the creation of consciousness and thought; they are the means of discernment and power, since they are essential to the act of comparison. Yet carried to an extreme, they present the danger of what Whitehead termed the evil of trivialization.[3] Existence is thoroughly relational, with those relations being internal to existence. The more open an entity is to a positive feeling of the many relations affecting it, the richer the experience of the entity will be. Manyness provides the basis for contrast and intensity, moving to high grades of existence. Too drastic a use of negation relative to the data of the past narrows the alternatives for what one can become, and hence affects the future as well. The richnesss of contrast is lost, resulting in a trivialization of experience. For low-grade entities, such trivialization may be no more than a stability of existence; but for high-grade entities, capable of entertaining many contrasts and hence of achieving complexity and intensity, the trivialization is measured against a "might-have-been" and is accordingly loss. In such a case, the loss can be experienced as evil either by the entity itself or by the societies which are themselves lessened by the poverty of the entity's contribution. Negative prehensions thus have the ambiguity of being necessary to the good of consciousness but also entailed in the trivialization of existence.

The extreme use of positive prehensions, more commonly called feelings by Whitehead, also carries a danger. If one is affected by one's entire past, and that past contains conflicting values relative to each other or to one's own desires for becoming, then to include as much as possible of that past within one's becoming opens one to the evil of discord, or the sense of unreconcilable alternatives. The power of negation can lessen the discord, but at the cost of closing oneself to much possible richness still available through one's past. Thus there is a tension between positive and negative prehensions in that they must provide a balance, but either used to an extreme can bring about triviality or discord with its attendant interpretations of evil.

Whitehead's third naming of evil was that of mental perceptions of excluded relevant alternatives. This differs from the exclusion of alternative possibilities, since in that case, the exclusion was the choice of the entity, whereas the mental perceptions of excluded relevant alternatives have to do with a forced exclusion. The reference is to ideals which, though suggested by a situation, are nevertheless problematic in that situation. They are ideals born out of season in a time not yet ripe for their fullest realization.[4] The ambiguity of this as an element of evil is that the vision of an as yet inapplicable ideal may create anguish and impatience with actuality, but by the same token, such a situation becomes the motivating power toward achievement of a different actuality. The power of visualizing alternatives, particularly in entities of high grades of consciousness, is a mixture of good and evil, given the other aspects of evil already mentioned.

A concrete illustration of this form of evil comes from consideration of the long history of the oppression of women. Virginia Lieson Brereton and Christa Ressmeyer Klein detail the history of women seeking ordination in their essay, "American Women in Ministry: A History of Protestant Beginning Points," published in *Women of Spirit*. Our illustration from their essay is as follows:

Anna Oliver and Anna Howard Shaw both sought permission for ordination from the Methodist Episcopal Church Conference in 1880. After the conference refused to act on the issue, only Oliver continued her struggle. By the time her financially weak congregation collapsed in 1883, her health was broken, and she died nine years later. Shaw, who had successfully sought ordination in the smaller Methodist Protestant Church, was so embittered that she soon ceased to care about the churches and turned her attention to the suffrage movement.[5]

Both women responded to an ideal for themselves which was thwarted by the prevailing mores of society. In choosing that ideal, they eschewed other possibilities for existence which would have been more pleasing to their cultural contemporaries. For them, the ideal was a good; for most of their contemporaries, it was deemed as an evil. Oliver was broken by the social response, which destroyed not only her pleasure in the ideal but also her possibility of realizing it. The implication is that her dedication to this one goal was such that she could not adapt to another, and she died disillusioned. Shaw was damaged in a different way: her adherence to a socially unacceptable ideal gave way to an alternative, but at the cost of embitterment. Thus both women illustrate the evil in experience when the ideal yearned for is not realizable.

One hundred years later, the ideal toward which each woman strove with such unhappy results is an actuality in the lives of many women ordained to ministry within the United Methodist Church, which is the successor body to both denominations. The efforts of Oliver and Shaw, while of little effect so far as they were concerned, nonetheless surely contributed to the slow change in society whereby other women can serve where they could not. In the brief story of their own lives, they were unsuccessful, whereas in the longer story of the hundred years, they were successful. Relative to themselves, there is a finality in the story; relative to other women, the story continues with a transforming power to bring new possibilities into existence. There is therefore an ambiguity in this form of evil, for it is, as Whitehead says, an "intermingling of Beauty and Evil."[6] It is both loss and gain.

Each of these three principles which Whitehead has used to elaborate upon his root definition of evil, "destruction as a dominant fact in the experience," is an essential component of every element of existence: every entity is finite, it involves exclusion of alternative possibilities, and it is open to the effect of alternatives not its own. Each one of these principles yields the richness of existence: finitude is the locus of value, and that value is achieved by selection. Insofar as entities are open to as yet unrealizable alternatives, novelty enters into existence with its own evolutionary rewards. The principles are good; finitude is good. And yet precisely these conditions of finitude allow evil as well as good into existence. To this degree, Whitehead's understanding of evil conforms to the objective pole wherein the root of evil is in the finite condition itself, yet with the fundamental ambiguity that the same structure which provides for evil is the structure which provides for good.[7]

One might consider, in such a situation, that it is choice which makes the difference, and thus that while evil is rooted in the finite condition the primary cause of actualized rather than possible evil rests with individual choices.[8] And there is indeed choice in the Whiteheadian universe: finitude involves an exclusion, a choice of alternatives, and this function is not restricted to humanity, but describes the dynamics of all existence. Electrons and protons become this, and not that, and the "thisness" they become involves a degree of indeterminacy which is resolved by the elements themselves. On the human level, the degree of alternatives increases, and the indeterminacy accordingly becomes better named as freedom.

The freedom is relative to the condition of finitude, but it is freedom nonetheless, so that the final reason for what a thing becomes is to be found both within that thing and within the conditions from which it arose. Thus the subjective pole of freedom is as involved in the metaphysics of evil as is the objective pole of finitude. However, to say that choice resolves the ambiguity of good and evil, explaining the one rather than the other, is too strong. To reduce the fact of evil to the myriad choices making up the ongoing universe is to overlook the inevitability of conflict when choices necessarily involve exclusion. thus the ambiguity of existence relative to good and evil is real, and the fundamental root of evil in a Whiteheadian understanding must hold both poles together: the subjective pole of choice and the objective pole of finitude are together the root of evil.

For all of this, finitude is the arena where value, be it good or evil, comes to existence; were it not for finitude, there would be neither good nor evil. As Whitehead put it:

All realization of the Good is finite, and necessarily excludes certain other types.[9]

All value is the gift of finitude which is the necessary condition for activity. ... Infinitude is mere vacancy apart from its embodiment of finite values.[10]

Goodness, to be good, can be no abstract category: it must have existence. Existence implies definiteness, so that the existent thing is one thing, and not another. This is finitude, boundedness, a givenness, which is as much what it is by what it has excluded as by what it has included. Thus finitude is necessary for the existence of that which is good. Yet finitude is also necessary for the existence of evil.

If finitude is the prerequisite of value, be it good or evil, can finitude be said to be neutral with regard to value? The earlier discussion of value and possibilities in reference to Schleiermacher is as relevant to a Whiteheadian system as to Schleiermacher's. There we suggested that possibilties, being abstract, are neither good nor evil in themselves; they must be contextually evaluated. For example, hatred as a possibility is simply that—the possibility of hatred. Its value must be judged relative to context. What is it that is being hated? Under what circumstances? For example, God is sometimes portrayed as hating evil, in which case one might assume hatred to be a good and godly thing. Yet hatred is also a motivating factor in many a destructive deed, in which case, one might call it evil. Hatred per se is neither good nor evil, but simply an abstract possibility for feeling. Hatred as possibility is neutral with regard to value, requiring the concreteness of existence for its valuation.

Existence, however, is no abstraction; it is the place of value, and therefore cannot be neutral with regard to value. Further, in a Whiteheadian system, existence far from being value-free is weighted toward the good. In and for itself, the general tendency for actuality is toward that which it measures as a good; in and for its relationships with others, this goodness becomes qualified so that degrees of goodness and evil become applicable to the valuation of the entity. The freedom involved in an entity's own becoming and the community within which that entity takes its place become two poles which must be taken together in a Whiteheadian understanding of good and evil.

With regard to an entity in and for itself, and the basis for claiming that this tends toward good, we must briefly discuss what is involved in the entity's coming into being. "An entity is actual, when it has significance for itself," we are told in the first section of *Process and Reality*,[11] where Whitehead discusses the categories pertinent to an analysis of existence. Impelled by a past and an ideal for its future, an entity comes to birth by reaching selectively into its past for that which is meaningful to it. The process of its becoming is a unification in terms of value: data from the past are contrasted and compared in a dynamic feeling for the possibilities of harmony inherent within that data. The final selection of actual unification is a decisive narrowing of the many possibilities to the one actuality. The principle of selectivity is the desire toward the immediate and more distant future: immediate with reference to one's own becoming, and more distant with reference to the feeling for how one's own decision will affect successors. Thus the entire coming to be of the entity is a positive valuation, a significance so deep that the entity becomes the value it chooses: it is finally the embodiment of the value; the entity is its decision. "We become like that which we love," is an ancient proverb; on the level of that basic element of being as analyzed by Whitehead, it has quite a literal application. An entity simply is its decision. Therefore, in a consideration of value, the significance for itself which determines an entity's actuality requires an initial positive valuation of finitude.

An important qualifier to this methphysical analysis is the reality which Whitehead noted and many a person will witness: The best can be bad. There can be a "remorseless working of things" in which circumstances of societal and personal history can render all possibilities as equally unbearable from the perspective of the subject. Endurance itself may be denied, and death preferred to conformity to conditions pressed upon one. Is there in such cases a positive valuation of finitude, an orientation toward the good? The witness to the goodness of existence in such tragedies is only the bitter comparison which provides judgment upon the present. The very decision to end one's life is an acknowledgment of a good belonging to existence, but not considered attainable within one's own. Were there no measure between what is and what might be, the conditions for suicide would not exist. Thus even the negation of one's own existence is a tragic witness to the value of existence in general.[12]

No actuality's value can be determined solely upon its own grounds in a relational universe. The necessary next step in evaluation, the contextual understanding which qualifies that original good is implicit in the very coming to be of an entity that develops from the many and toward the many. Relationships are integral to an entity's being, so that these relationships form a natural and legitimate qualification, be it up or down, of the initial valuation of the entity. The entity is a decision of value made possible through its relatedness to a world of beings and becomings beyond itself, so that the final evaluation of the entity requires this larger world of relatedness. The norm for judging the entity in this realm derives from this very interdependence. Since an entity aims at intensity of significance for itself, insofar as this aim is fostered by the possibilities made available to it by another, that other entity, *in this relationship,* is good; insofar as its aim is hindered by the other, that other, *in this relationship,* is deemed evil. Insofar as others are considered irrelevant to the entity, they are neither necessarily good nor evil, but simply there. The same situation holds with reference to entities which succeed this particular event: insofar as the actualized entity enhances value for future entities, to those entities it is a good; insofar as it decreases value, it will be experienced as evil. The complexity which must be noted in this multiple valuation is precisely its multiple nature. There is no single valuation of an entity; its value is named from as many perspectives as it has relationships. And those relationships, in a Whiteheadian universe, extend throughout the universe. Therefore, an actualized, finite being in and for itself generally tends toward the self-perceived good; insofar as it is an existence for others, or a being in relationship, it will tend toward varying degrees of good and evil.[13] But the intitial weight is toward the good.

The "freedom in community" by which we have designated this Whiteheadian way of understanding good and evil is just this point and counterpoint of the entity for itself and for others. The entity must be both by its very nature; there is no arbitrary imposition of the community upon the individual. The relation to others is essential to every being, and, therefore, one's meaning or goodness or evil must finally be reckoned not on the basis of the single entity alone, but upon the basis of the entity and its relationships.[14] An entity is free to choose from the many possibilities made available to it from relationships offered through its past. Thus its freedom derives from a community which has defined its realm of alternatives. Its limitations are its boundaries which make particular possibilities relevant—and, therefore, real and actualizable. Likewise, the final decision which marks the entity is, in its turn, a formation of possibilities for future becomings. Freedom and community, one and many, operating in a rhythmic togetherness, are the very fabric of actuality and, therefore, of value; both dimensions are required for a full accounting of good and evil.

Whitehead offers both concrete and abstract discussions of this contextual understanding of good and evil. By way of further illustration, we will consider the reference in *Religion in the Making* to an instance of human degradation, and the essay, "Mathematics and the Good," wherein Whitehead develops the implications of the entire pattern of relationships for the understanding of good.

The passage from *Religion in the Making* centers around the following:

A hog is not an evil beast, but when man is degraded to the level of a hog, with the accompanying atrophy of finer elements, he is no more evil than a hog. The evil of the final degradation lies in the comparison of what is with what might have been. During the process of degradation, the comparison is an evil for the man himself, and at its final stage it remains an evil for others ... The evil lies in the loss to the social environment.[15]

The case is that wherein an individual chooses to actualize a value which is less than the best which was open. The best refers to those finer elements which have been discarded. Their qualitative difference from their lesser rivals lies in the loss of intensity which is entailed in their rejection. A possible richness of existence is sacrificed for a lower form, with a consequent loss to the future which is dependent to some degree upon its inheritance from this particular entity. The passage illustrates the "exclusion of alternative possibility" as evil which was discussed earlier.

Yet it must be noticed that "when a man is degraded to the level of a hog...he is no more evil than a hog." The final decisions of the man are accepted for what they are: there is no penalty involved in the rejection of his finer possibilities other than those which are natural, and which may not even be felt as penalties to the individual concerned. While we might consider the lower plane of existence a form of penalty, it is after all self-imposed, and, therefore, represents the final valuation of the individual at that particular moment of decision. The individual has been free to actualize this form of existence as well as the higher, and the actualization is accepted for what it is. "He is no more evil than a hog." This bespeaks the radical freedom of creativity given in Whitehead. It is no longer the case that an essence is given to which the creature must conform or face a punitive rejection; rather, the creature is free to become what it can and will within its parameters of possibility. This freedom of creativity means that the creature assumes a radical responsibility for choices which are made, since one chooses the essential value which one ultimately becomes. This value is accepted, and becomes part of the stream of being which influences the future. But just in this movement toward the future, wherein the pole of freedom moves into the relational responsibility for community, we see the area of evil, which "lies in loss to the social environment."

Freedom is held in relation to community. The occasions which succeed those who have responsibly chosen a lower form of existence than was possible find their own possibilities toward a high achievement significantly lowered through the poverty of the past. Yet the rejected ideal which was significant for the past retains the shadow of its significance for the future, since every feeling "retains the impress of what it might have been, but is not" (PR 227).

This comparison of the "might have been" with the actual weight of influence of the alternative achievement creates conflict for the relevant becoming entities, as was illustrated earlier through the examples of Oliver and Shaw. To those who feel the loss with the greatest keenness, the loss is a positive evil. The initial occasions themselves are responsible for this effect upon the future; the larger community is responsible for how it deals with this effect. The evil itself stems from this contextual situation of relationships.

In "Mathematics and the Good," Whitehead gives considerable attention to the overall pattern of relationships and their significance for good or evil. The major point of the essay revolves around the essential relatedness of each individual to the entire universe, such that "every item derives its truth, and its very meaning, from its unanalyzed relevance to the background which is the unbounded Universe.... There is no entity which enjoys an isolated self-sufficiency of existence. In other words, finitude is not self-supporting."[16]

This last statement requires two interpretations. First, the finite reality is a dependent reality, requiring relationships for existence, as has already been shown. Yet there is also this: Finite reality, moving ever into new realizations of value, draws upon an infinity of possibility. In its actualization of one value from the infinite many, finitude meets infinity, infusing it with concretness, with vividness, with the exclusive value of actuality. The realm of the finite, then, depends upon the infinite for the very possibilities which come into being; but conversely, the infinite depends upon the finite for the full realization of its meaning. Infinity in itself is vacuous, diffuse, all-inclusive, undefined. Finitude in itself, apart from the infinity of possibilities, would fall into static repetition of discreteness. What actually obtains in the reality of existence, in a manner reminiscent of Hegel, is this meeting of infinity and finitude, this unlimited pouring of richness into vital existence.

However, the very unlimitedness of this increasing finite sphere, and the relatedness which ties every actuality into all others, means that this coming into existence of infinite possibilities creates a pattern whose intricacies of relationships are ever playing over the surface with unspoken hints of new depths. Each new actuality represents, through its relationships, a qualification of all others— the Leibnitian insistence that the whole is required for the evaluation of each part is most relevant here. The very vastness of this network of meaning pushes these constantly becoming creative relationships to "depths and distances below and beyond appearance."[17] The pattern of infinity in finitude becomes a changing panorama of beauty wherein each part plays multiple roles in relation to the whole. It is this pattern of the universe, unreachable by the abstractions of human reason, and yet intuited through those mathematical patterns which witness to the magnitude of the relationships, which becomes for Whitehead the most adequate notion of the Good.[18].

In *Adventures of Ideas*, Whitehead speaks of the universal pattern more specifically in terms of zest, beauty, truth, adventure, art, and peace. These qualities are not arbitrarily imposed upon the pattern of relationships in the world, but are derived from the advance of novelty in the process of the world whereby the world is brought to more complex and richer modes of existence. Process, insofar as we observe it, is directional; there is an "advance of the temporal world."[19] The advance is to just the increased complexity of existence which is delineated through Whitehead's detailed consideration of zest, beauty, truty, adventure, art, and peace. The pattern, then, becomes quite definitely a unity, a harmony, embracing all existence and impelling it toward new modes of union between the infinite and the finite.

How does this abstract concept of a pattern, which at first seems to relegate all problems of evil to the realm of aesthetics, wherein discord contrasts with and therefore contributes to the dominant theme of harmony, affect the concrete instances of evil? The effect lies quite directly in the increasing complexity of relationships which forbids the finality of any evil. If the entity in itself is a good, and if evil becomes the product of a relationship insofar as the entity has a deleterious effect upon others, then surely the full scope of those meaningful relationships is required for the most adequate understanding of the meaning of the original entity. The abstract notion of the pattern of the universe is not merely aesthetic, important as this dimension is to Whitehead, for it finally speaks to the concrete meaning of each and every entity: the universe is the scope of its relationships. Insofar as new entities continually come into existence, the ramifications of meaning are quite literally never-ending. Thus the "community" aspect of freedom-in-community is an infinite pole in an unbounded universe. The evil of any one relationship can never be the last word.

While one might indeed consider the universe the context of determining the value of any one entity, this can only be done responsibly by dealing with entities within increasingly complex societies. That is, though the universe is the context, there are many steps between the individual entity and this full determination of meaning. The steps involve relation to societies of increasing scope, and the judgment not only of individuals, but of individual societies and societies of societies. For example, many entities make a person, who in turn is part of a social grouping, that in turn relates significantly to a more inclusive community, and so on. The value of communities as well as the value of individuals is to be judged finally not simply in terms of self-significance, but in terms of significance for others in the increasingly wider communities of the world and universe.

We began this discussion of the Whiteheadian concept of evil by relating a significant passage from *Adventures of Ideas* to three dimensions of evil: perpetual perishing, a competition of values resulting in a self-selected exclusion of possibilities, and a competition of values resulting in an other-imposed exclusion of possibilities. All three relate to loss, whether of existence itself, of meaning, or of ideals. These latter two modes of loss were then illustrated in the reference from *Religion in the Making,* with this concrete reference related to the whole context of the necessarily abstract pattern of the good as given in "Mathematics and the Good." But it is seen that the application of that notion of the total pattern to the individual entity or society answers at least two of the dimensions of evil, that is, the destruction of meaning and of the ideal. The continuous intensification and modification of meaning can work toward the transformation of those meanings which originally were felt as evil. The same is true with the evil which relates to the felt loss of an ideal. When this loss is set within the larger framework of the expanding community which is the universe, then the ideal retains its significance. Although it may have been lost in time and place to the one, be it individual or society or epoch, the ideal's very impact of "lostness" leaves its imprint on the ongoing process, and this witness may yet be its means of transition from pure ideality to the finite feeling of value in some future reality.[20]

This relational understanding of evil as following inevitably from freedom in community embraces both poles of the tradition. Like Augustine and others emphasizing the subjective root of evil in the will, the freedom of each entity to act within given limitations and possibilities gives responsibility to the individual for its actions and, to a degree, their effects. But the contextual aspect of freedom is precisely that realm of the objective pole named by Leibniz, or the conditions of finitude. Freedom is limited, not by one's perversity but by one's relationships, be they to one's own past, to family and friends, to society, or to nature. This relational context provides the ground for naming reality good or evil, and thus the objective and subjective poles of evil are held in tension, each qualifying the other.

This tension will prove both problematic and creative. By naming both poles as implicated in the ground of evil, problems for over-coming evil are raised with some acuteness. And yet precisely because both poles are fundamental, the Whiteheadian theory of freedom in community allows an expression of the dynamics involved in each of the effects of evil named in the various systems considered in our earlier chapters. We will first relate this theory of evil to these other systems, and in subsequent chapters we will confront the problems which are raised within the Whiteheadian system for any meaningful form of redemption from evil.

Kant defined moral evil within the realm of freedom and finitude: one must, but does not, conform to the moral law implanted within human nature. Whitehead's correspondence to the implanted, a priori moral law would be the actual entity's initial sense of that which it ought to be. As will be developed in later chapters, Whitehead locates the source for each entity's highest good as God. The function of God within his system grows from an initial understanding of a principle of unrest, accounting for the creativity of things, to a principle of limitation, accounting for order rather than chaos. Finally, in the concluding pages of *Process and Reality*, God emerges as fully manifesting all of the dynamics of the actual entity, and hence functioning with consciousness and purpose in the world. God is the orderer of possibilities, adjudicating their relevance to the becoming world, influencing the world toward its own individual/communal good.[21] Thus the effect of God upon every entity is to give that entity an initial direction for its own becoming which is adjusted to the circumstances of the entity. It is a real rather than a theoretical possibility, and is "best" in terms of the actuality of the entity's context. Further, the aim is proposed rather than imposed. With these important qualifications, the mechanics of moral failure in Whitehead are very similar to those in Kant. On the macrocosmic level of the society of entities constituting the human soul, failure with regard to one's best possibilities rests solely with the responsi-bility of the person. Like Kant, Whitehead retains an inherent ability within the person to conform to the standard of the initial aim. This is due to the relativity of the aim, fitted to a situation with all of its exigencies taken into account. Unlike Kant, there is no built-in necessity that one will fail to act according to the presented aim. In this respect, Whitehead's system is more Pelagian than Kant's.[22] The Pelagianism is mitigated by the necessarily conditioned nature of the aim; the "best" relative to a particular situation might be "worst" by a less restricted measure. That is, no individual faces a value-free possibility since at the point of choice, value is conditioned by context. This relativity of the standard fits the standard to the person's circumstances; it is an attainable goal. This heightens the responsibility of the person to adopt the highest good possible in that situation. Kant's action according to a categorical rule had to issue in failure; Whitehead's influence toward a relative rule can issue in success. This possibility of success is the basis for the radical responsibility within Whitehead's system. The given nature of the good, the freedom of a person relative to that good, and the responsibility to enact the good—each of these is fundamental to Kant's perception of moral evil, and each has its counterpart in process philosophy.

The relationship of Whitehead to the insights of Schleiermacher is established through the notion of incompletion and self-creativity. The former denotes an interrelatedness of being which is fundamental to both philosophies. Schleiermacher portrayed a world of responsive activity, wherein all being was characterized as interdependent. Evil arose from the creative action of individuals within the situation of mutual dependence: insofar as action complemented the welfare of beings, goodness was realized, but failure in this regard created evil. Thus the possibility for evil stemmed from the basic incompletion of individual existence; actual evil resulted from misused creativity relative to a particular finite situation. While Whitehead's terminology differs, he yields the same insights. The interdependence of being is firmly established in the very constitution of the actual entity, which is a unification of relationships and a thrust toward new relationships. Incompletion in process thought speaks of this need of the entity for that which is beyond itself, the insufficiency of any entity in itself alone.

Also like Schleiermacher, Whitehead conceives of a creature which participates in creation, forging its values through the possibilities which are available to it. Evil originates in the clash of values and the destruction of being, be it physical or moral. Physically this is simply perishing, while morally it is the lessening of existence through the impoverishment of one's own or another's maximum possibilities. This evil is neither directly attributable to finitude nor to possibilities in themselves, but relates to the creative decision of an entity in its effects within a larger society. Thus the understanding of evil derived from Schleiermacher receives it complement in Whitehead, so that a theory of redemption worked out in Whiteheadian categories speaks as well to the needs presented through Schleiermacher, regardless of deep differences which present incompatibilities in other areas of their respective systems.

Like Hegel, Whitehead has a sweeping cosmic vision of existence. For both relationality is a key, with Hegel relating the Absolute Spirit to its realization in human history. For Hegel there is a teleological progression of history; while this is less worked out in Whitehead, he nevertheless utilizes as a key concept "the creative advance of nature." Much work has been done, notably by George Lucas, in developing the similarities and contrasts between the two systems.[23] With regard to evil, for Hegel there was a tension between one's individual passions, and the teleological aim of the universal. The corollary in Whitehead is the sense in which the individual is no isolated finality, but inescapably relational. It is both for itself and for others; what it is in and for itself has an inexorable effect upon others. There is then a tension when that which is considered good for the self works against the best interests of others. Responsibility in this system is multiple: one is responsible for oneself and for the effects on others insofar as others must deal with that which has been given through this self. While the two goods may be consonant, there is no metaphysical necessity that this be so.

There is also in Hegel the sense of alienation in a necessary separation of the individual as a basis for the reconciliation with the universal. The separation is alienating, since it entails a sense of belonging to that which is other than the self. The echo to this in Whitehead is again the integral nature of relationships. The entity becomes a particular amidst a sea of connectedness. Prehension involves the transmission of energy, so that which is "there" is felt "here." There *is* a belongingness beyond the self—and yet the self comes into being in separation from others, in the privacy of its own becoming. While the Whiteheadian development of this would not use "alienation" as a term—there is, after all, a *transmission* of feeling —the dynamics are indeed those of separation, so that evil interpreted along Hegelian lines can be addressed with coherence within a Whiteheadian system.

The problem of meaninglessness given through Nietzsche hinges ultimately upon the problem of the loss of transcendence. When the individual alone is the ground of meaning, then meaning cannot long endure, for it shares in the transitoriness of the individual. If the meaning is extended to the world at large, the fate is nevertheless the same, for the world is likewise perishing in its temporality. Nietzsche scorned the concern over the threat to meaning which this loss of transcendence implies, and he sought instead a new establishment of meaning through joyful acceptance of this condition, demonstrated through self-affirmation and creativity. Yet ultimately Nietzsche too grounds this new source of meaning in the pseudo-transcendence first of the will, and then of the eternal return. Even while he scorned the problem, he appears to have felt constrained to find a solution.

Whitehead's relation to a Nietzschean form of evil is primarily through the reintroduction of transcendence so that the problem can be met.[24] However, the possibilities for a solution to the problem of transitoriness—and, therefore, meaning—are not antithetical to the insights which are closest to the heart of Nietzsche's analysis. Self-affirmation is echoed in the very definition of actuality as that which has significance for itself; self-creativity is fundamental to process; and surely the affirmation of the past has a sympathetic correspondence in the requirement that every entity must take account of its entire past in one way or another. Thus despite the great differences between Nietzsche and Whitehead, the fundamental conditions of a creative reality which is the world is equally important in both philosophies. This shared interest becomes a point of contact, so that the Whiteheadian mode of transcendence, which we will develop in the next four chapters, can speak to the problem uncovered by Nietzsche.

We began this chapter by listing a number of threats to individual and societal existence in our own time: holocaust, apartheid, nuclear winter, environmental destruction, poverty, hunger, terrorism, and war. Each is a witness to a situation of freedom in community, where individual actions have societal effects. Consequently, each is a witness to social responsibility. In the first pair, holocaust and apartheid, the good of one group is maintained at the expense of the good of another; social relatedness and responsibility are denied. In the second pair, the interrelatedness of humanity with its environment is given scant notice, with the disastrous results being not only the destruction of the environment, but also the destruction of the human species insofar as humanity is dependent upon the health of the environment. In poverty and hunger, the dependence of the individual on the environment which must sustain us is likewise implicated, as is the mutual responsibility of human beings to regard themselves as interrelated, or as Kant would have it, as an "ethical commonwealth." Finally, terrorism and war likewise speak to the competition of values in a finite sphere, and the ability through our very interdependence to bring destruction rather than goodness upon each other. To the degree that any portion of the human community is destroyed, every human being suffers to a greater or lesser degree. Each of the evils named can be understood through the violation of an interdependence that is neither accidental nor arbitrary, but which is the very stuff of all existence. Freedom in community is the structure which allows evil to occur; freedom in community is also the structure which allows redemption to occur.

Thus the elements which compose the contemporary sensitivity to evil can be gathered together in a Whiteheadian analysis of existence, so that the components of freedom in community developed through his thought can provide the context whereby evil is understood. The now radical freedom and openness of finitude become the possibility of a moral evil which is contextual, pertaining to relationships, and a metaphysical evil which relates to the necessity of excluded alternatives, incompleteness, and perpetual perishing. Both moral and metaphysical forms of evil must be answered in a theory of the overcoming of evil; the basis of this overcoming must be found not only in history, but also in transcendence, or in the nature of a redemptive God.

V

Subjective Immortality

Freedom in community gives rise to evil; freedom in community also gives rise to good. The structure of relationships is such that existence is fragile, vulnerable to dangers and destruction mediated through the necessary openness to relationships—and yet this very openness is the source of strength and richness, since relationships also mediate communal good to the individual, and offer a completion of meaning. This creates an inescapable ambiguity with regard to good and evil, for relationality is at once the structure through which evil occurs, and the structure through which redemption occurs.

Therefore, there can be no full overcoming of evil within the historical process of the world. The very nature of evil in the relationality of freedom and finitude is such that evil in principle cannot be answered fully in finite circumstances—the overcoming of evil in history is always partial. At that, the partiality is unevenly distributed; there are those whose lives are permanently distorted through societal or personal evil, such that they do not or cannot benefit from the good which is accomplished despite their suffering. Only if those partial triumphs over evil in history may be read as intimations of an order where all evil is everlastingly overcome is it legitimate to conceive of any full answer to evil, or of God as the final overcomer of evil.[1] If the finality of destruction remains as an unrefuted witness to the supremacy of evil in even one instance, then good exists in eternal duality with an evil it could not—or would not—overcome.

81

Thus in order to formulate an adequate answer to evil, we are forced to consider not only the dynamics of a redemption within this world, but to extend our consideration toward an ultimate overcoming which lies beyond our immediate experience in the world. The thesis of these remaining chapters is that it is possible to develop a coherent theory of such everlasting redemption through the process categories of Whitehead, and furthermore, that such everlastingness is the ground of historical redemption.[2] Redemption beyond history is a basis for hope within history, affecting what is possible in history. Thus we will first develop the possibility of subjective immortality and everlasting redemption within a Whiteheadian system, and then explore their connections with the ongoing historical process. These developments will necessarily build on and toward a process concept of God as the overcomer of evil, so that our final chapter will explicate the dynamics of such a God.

The notion of subjective immortality builds upon the relationship between God and the world according to the process dynamics of existence. These dynamics were developed partially in Chapter IV, although the language there was somewhat balanced between Whitehead's technical usage and ordinary usage. To develop so speculative a notion as immortality requires a careful use of key Whiteheadian concepts: prehension, subjective immediacy, concrescence, satisfaction, objective immortality, creativity, and the primordial/consequent nature of God.

Chapter IV noted that every finite reality exists through relationships: a subject is evoked into becoming by the energy of past actualizations. What the subject becomes depends upon three things: the actual limitations imposed by the past for the particular standpoint of the becoming occasion, the real transcendence of that past provided by novel but relevant possibilities, and the creative decision of the subject with regard to its own unification of actuality and possibility. The actual becoming of the subject is what is meant by concrescence and subjective immediacy: concrescence refers to the process of unification, and subjective immediacy, to the experience of that process. Satisfaction refers to the completion of the process. Since immediacy is a function of concrescence, the satisfaction is devoid of subjective immediacy.

The subject emerges in concrescence, beginning with feelings of data from the past, or the given actual world. These feelings are termed prehensions by Whitehead, so that the subject prehends the data of the past. The subject also prehends or feels the possibilities for its own future. Through the unification of these, which requires a contrasting and evaluating until the complexity is reduced to a simpler unity, the subject creates itself in the present. This move-ment can also be called a progression from the physical pole (actu-ality), through the mental pole (possibility), toward the concrete unity of the two, which is the creation of a new actuality (often called an actual occasion of experience, or more simply, an occasion).

Once the becoming is complete, Whitehead holds that subjectivity perishes, but effectiveness in the future begins. This effectiveness is designated as "objective immortality," for now the completed entity is itself the past as object, ready to influence the immediate and distant future. The entire process, whether subjective or objective, is creative. In the first instance, it is creative as the unification of actuality and possibility, or what Whitehead terms concrescent creativity; and in the second instance, it is creative as it evokes a new becoming, or what Whitehead terms transitional creativity (often simply called the superjective nature of the occasion).

This model is intended to describe the dynamics of all existence at its most fundamental level. While it can be used descriptively as a model of our own integrally relational psychological nature, its primary purpose is to provide a model for understanding the "build-ing blocks" of our multifaceted existence. Persons are "societies" of these actual entities, with perhaps a particular governing "strand" of these occasions constituting what we call "soul."

We will expand these initial descriptions as each is actually used in development of the case for subjective immortailty. For the present, we must give an equally brief description of the process dynamics applied to God. While our final chapter will give a detailed discussion of the reasons and structure of these dynamics, each of these three chapters dealing with the overcoming of evil will build toward that extended discussion of the metaphysics of the process notion of God.

Whitehead's complex understanding of God, like his understand-ing of all actuality, is bipolar—God, too, must have a physical pole and a mental pole, referring to the feeling of completed actualities and to the feeling of possibilities, respectively. However, in God there is a reversal of the polar structure, for reasons which will be more fully developed in Chapter VIII. This reversal yields a qualitative differ-ence between God and the world, even though the actual categories of process apply to both. Every temporal actuality begins from the physical pole with the feelings of a complete actual world which admits of no addition. Its possibilities for its own becoming are limited to forms of transcendence relevant to that past. Thus there is a given priority to the physical pole and the past. The reversal of the poles in the divine nature gives the priority to possibilities, or the mental pole. These possibilities are timeless, unlimited by any past, and are envisaged by God in an order relative to themselves, apart from any reference to actuality. This constitutes God's eternal and unbounded primordial nature, and provides the ground for God's total openness to all actuality. God, moving from an infinite openness of possibilities, concresces through prehension of every completed actuality. Whereas the world of completed actualities functions as a past for becoming finite entities, the same actualities are more like a future to God. Past and future are reversed for God and the world.

God's openness to the world is the physical pole of God, called the consequent nature. It is consequent upon the eternal primordial vision of possibilities, and also consequent upon the reality of what comes to be in the world. This is the temporal aspect of God, and it is in principle always incomplete and increasing. Thus the reversal of the poles in God means that God, unlike the world, is an everlasting entity, always becoming and yet always complete. The unity of God is the integration of the primordial and consequent natures in what we will suggest is a continually dynamic satisfaction.

With this brief background, we proceed to the discussion of objective and subjective immortality. The concept of subjective immortality itself is not used by Whitehead, but it seems to haunt the edges of his system as he struggled with the insufficiency of objective immortality alone in relation to the reality of perishing.[3]

But objective immortality within the temporal world does not solve the problem set by the penetration of the finer religious intuition. 'Everlastingness' has been lost; and 'everlastingness' is the content of that vision upon which the finer religions are built—the 'many' absorbed everlastingly in the final unity (PR 268).

Objective immortality, or the occasion's effect on the future, contributes to the perishing of the subject in two ways. First, it signals the perishing of the immediacy of the subject itself; and second, it is itself subject to negation by the new present, and to an eventual fading away in the ongoing supersession of events.

Whitehead establishes the principle of objective immortality in the four categories of explanation dealing with the way one entity functions in the creation of another, stating that "it belongs to every 'being' that it is a potential for every 'becoming.'"[4] Following its own concrescence, an entity's creativity becomes transitional, like "the transference of throbs of emotional energy."[5] This means that the results of becoming are now made available for further becomings, and that the creativity whereby an entity has become passes over into an impetus for the future. There is no limit to the number of future occasions which a completed occasion may influence; the completed occasion is in this sense immortal. But its "thereness" for immortality is devoid of subjective immediacy; with the conclusion of its own concrescence, immediacy—like the creativity which it embodies—passes into the new present. The concluded concrescence is thus immortal as an object.

Subjectivity is superseded by objectivity; this maintains the givenness of the past, with this givenness being requisite for order to be attained by each succeeding actual occasion. The givenness is established by the determinate satisfactions, devoid of subjective immediacy, allowing for future accounting. Whitehead holds that the objectivity of the past allows prehension by the becoming present, and this is objective immortality. The concept is thus foundational in process philosophy.

How, then, can we possibly assign the continuance of immediacy into satisfaction, along with the possibility of subjective immortality? Subjectivity and immortality are so far discontinuous terms, the one beginning where the other ends. For the occasion, immortality begins with the enjoyment of satisfaction—an enjoyment which appears to belong not to the occasion which made the satisfaction available, but to a succeeding occasion in objective immortality, for "no actual entity can be conscious of its own satisfaction; for such knowledge would be a component in the process, and would thereby alter the satisfaction" (PR 85). Subjectivity can claim only the ideal of the satisfaction as the occasion presses toward its actulization; its attainment is the occasion's death—unless we can render subjective immortality coherent.

In answer to this dilemma, we propose two moves: First, a reconsideration of creativity that will provide a deeper understanding of the dynamics of satisfaction; and second, a shift in perspective relative to objectivity and subjectivity. The first argument proceeds from the understanding of creativity as it relates to the occasions. We will explore the possibility that the satisfaction embodies creativity in an intermediate mode between concrescence and transition, holding the results of concrescence together in a dynamic union, and generating the the thrust toward the future which accounts for the emerging occasions.

Creativity, along with oneness and manyness, is an ultimate metaphysical term for Whitehead, one of the categories which underlies the development of every phase of his thought.[6] Creativity itself is therefore an explanatory and foundational principle; creativity is in no way to be understood as something that functions in addition to actual entities. There is no brooding, abstract quality which woos a world into being, no ghostly "thing" that becomes instantiated through one occasion after another. Creativity, in actuality, is inseparable from the entities of the process: "Every condition to which the process of becoming conforms in any particular instance has its reason *either* in the character of some actual entity in the actual world of that concrescence, *or* in the character of the subject which is in process of concrescence" (PR 24). Therefore, when Whitehead states at the conclusion of *Process and Reality* that "God and the World are the contrasted opposites in terms of which Creativity achieves its supreme task" (PR 348), the creativity to which he refers is in no way to be taken as something over and above either God or the world. Creativity is, and is only, in creative actual entities. The extreme importance of an awareness of this lies in the correction of any tendency to think of creativity as a thing in and of itself, for *all* creativity exists only as it is instantiated in particular actual entities.

Whitehead affirms this in referring to an entity as a subject-superject, for this term embraces creativity in its concrescent and transitional forms. The occasion creates itself in concrescence, and forces the emergence of a future beyond itself in transition.[7] Whitehead envisions this force toward the future as stemming from the internal completion of an occasion, its satisfaction. However, if satisfaction is considered as separate from the subjective immediacy of an occasion, so that it is itself a static completion devoid of any further activity, then is there not a question as to its ability to generate a transitional thrust of creativity toward a future? Could one not then see an ambiguity in the ground of creativity, seeing creativity as a force which leaves an occasion, and thus in some sense transcends it as an independent force apart from the actualities which give it form?

If the satisfaction of an occasion is divorced from creativity, and yet gives rise to a creative future, then creativity appears to be a "thing" that leaves one entity in order to bring another into being, as if it were a life force moving from entity to entity. Such a passage of creativity would be a passage of being, and God and the world could be considered to be in the grip of the ultimate metaphysical ground[8] in a concrete as well as in an abstract sense. If, on the other hand, the actual entity is creativity, and creativity is nothing other than the subjective activity of the entity,[9] why must creativity "leave" the entity upon its satisfaction? Why cannot creativity beget creativity without dying in the process—and indeed, is not a vital creativity rather than an exhausted creativity a more likely source of the thrust toward new occasions?

The usual answer to such questions is that creativity leaves an occasion because the occasion's active functioning has been brought to a conclusion. And yet this is not so; the occasion still functions for a future, although in terms of the givenness which it has created.[10] But must givenness be considered as wholly passive, or as static, in order to become stubborn fact for another? May not givenness also be givingness, in which case it may be stubborn fact, but not static at all?[11] Perhaps the given and giving nature of the "completed" occasion is itself a mode of creativity, intermediate between the concrescent and transitional phases. Such an intermediate mode may be considered through the following passage, despite the obvious contradiction to our proposal which it contains:

The notion of 'satisfaction' is the notion of the entity as concrete, abstracted from the process of concrescence; it is the outcome separated from the process, thereby losing the actuality of the atomic entity, which is both process and outcome (*PR* 84).

If the actuality of the atomic entity is *both* process and outcome, then in actuality, as opposed to the abstraction of analysis, the satisfaction of the occasion is the embodiment of its concrescence. The occasion is then the result together with its becoming, and it is this wholeness of process and outcome, rather than process alone, that constitutes the subjective immediacy of the occasion.[12] The satisfaction is defined as that final self-valuation of the entity whereby the diverse objects it has unified are held together as one. The diversity is not merged unidentifiably into a conglomerate whole, for if this were the case, coordinate analysis of the occasion through its satisfaction would be impossible. Rather, the satisfaction of the entity is the togetherness of a diversity, a manyness in one.[13] If, however, the final satisfaction is just this holding together, then why is it not as dynamic as the process of coming together in the first place? Indeterminateness is gone, that is so, but it is now replaced by the fullness of that which is fully actual. The activity is now not selection, but enjoyment, the dynamics of holding the many in unity. Given its activity, it is the culmination of the immediacy generated through concrescence. It is a conclusion to immediacy that is also the inclusion of immediacy, and not a conclusion bereft of that immediacy. Immediacy is becoming *and* satisfaction: the result, together with its becoming.

Whitehead's ambiguity on the point is his emphasis that an occasion cannot be conscious of its own satisfaction, on the grounds that this would require something akin to a prehension of the satisfaction, requiring a new unification. The occasion would then lose its givenness, becoming another, which by definition is a loss of immediacy, and entails the succession of occasions. However, in the view being developed here, the final enjoyment does not come within the category of prehension at all—it is the result of what has been done with prehensions. The satisfaction is not the occasion's transcendent overview of the results of its becoming; the satisfaction *is* the dynamic result of its becoming. Satisfaction *is* enjoyment, and, therefore, active rather than passive. Satisfaction is a form of creativity which then naturally gives rise to givingness, or the transitional power which offers just this mode of determinateness to a future, evoking that future into becoming a new present.

A further argument for creativity as enjoyment serving as an intermediate between creativity as concrescence and transition is that it provides a bridge between the two forms, giving new distinction to each. After all, that which is concrescent creativity from the perspective of one entity is transitional creativity from the perspective of another: prehension is transitional creativity, subjectively appropriated. One could argue, on this view, that there is *only* concrescent creativity, or *only* transitional creativity, depending upon whether one spoke from the perspective of the present or the past. If the satisfaction is active, not passive, and, therefore, embodies its own form of creativity as the experience of decision rather than the making of decision, this becomes the generation of the givingness which evokes the future. Creativity as enjoyment (or satisfaction) provides the breathing space of the universe, the rhythmic pause which creates the order of concluding and beginning, beginning, and concluding. Concrescence, enjoyment, and transition become the three phases of the creative advance of existence. Concrescence is the first mode of creativity, grounding the satisfaction which covers concrescence with the second mode, enjoyment of itself, which generates the third mode, the superjective offering of itself to its future. The enjoying occasion no longer prehends either itself or another; it does not reach toward another entity in order to objectify but rather to evoke potential entities into becoming actual. Enjoyment generates transition, givingness. This initial transition, combined with many likewise dynamic transitions from many satisfactions, inaugurates the becoming of the next occasion. As the many energies of transmission converge, they are transformed into concrescent creativity, or feelings reaching for unity through the creation of yet one more subject. In this phase, the feelings become selective prehensions, cutting away the many competing energies in the movement which is the new immediacy of the present creation.

As indicated earlier, the concrescence of an entity is its own generation of itself, so that its subjectivity is grounded in its concrescent activity. The satisfaction terminates this activity—it is as if for one shimmering moment the occasion becomes visible in actuality, embodying in a culminating intensity that value of its becoming. But the ground of that immediacy, the concrescence, is gone, so that the satisfaction has no basis for sustaining itself beyond that one appearance which is its addition to reality. The satisfaction is a hovering between attainment and perishing, during which it enjoys itself and offers itself.

If the satisfaction is truly creative in this sense of a dynamic holding together of many in a harmonious unification, then the transitional effect of the occasion is more coherent. Even as manyness has begotten a unity, so the unity gives rise to many through its own mode of creativity. Creativity does not leave the one, it is generated anew through the satisfaction of the one. Creativity does not move as the spirit over the waters, bringing now this and now that occasion into being; creativity moves generatively through actuality, increasing with actuality: "the many become one, and are increased by one" (PR 21).

Transitional creativity moves naturally from the embodied creativity of enjoyment. Implicit within the becoming of the occasion has been the awareness of many contemporaries, not explicitly in terms of their content, since these contemporaries are not prehended, but rather implicitly, through their foreshadowed presence in the occasion's prehended past. Thus the occasion develops, and is aware of so developing, in the context of a new multiplicity which is coming into being.

Any occasion will experience its past as 'anticipating' the prolongation of that type of order into the future beyond that past. But this future includes the occasion in question and its contemporary environment. In this way, there is an indirect immanence of its contemporary world in that occasion; not in respect to its particular individual occasions, but as the general substratum for that relation of order.... The contemporary world enters into experience as the passive subject of relations and qualities (AI 196).

The occasion's concern has been the unification of the manifold past into the oneness of itself; but this very concern for unification forces the occasion beyond itself to the concerns of a new unification made possible and made necessary by its own creative activity. Its moment of satisfaction is its moment of demand; its enjoyment of itself is its generation of another.[14]

The other comes into being through its feelings of the many now subjective satisfactions of the past, and this is the point in the argument where we must make the case that the satisfaction allows either subjective or objective prehension. Whether a prehension is objective or subjective depends not upon the satisfaction, but upon the prehending entity. We will argue that finite entities must objectify the satisfaction, so that in the temporal world only objective immortality obtains for the prehended entity. However, God has no need to objectify the satisfaction, so that God prehends the satisfaction's entirety, and hence its subjectivity.

This utilization of a shift in perspective to establish objective or subjective immortality is not antithetical to a Whiteheadian enterprise. In the final section of *Process and Reality*, Whitehead asserts a group of antitheses.[15] The truth of each component of an antithesis depends upon the perspective from which it is seen, for perspectives require a shift in the meaning of a phrase adapting it to the unique conditions of each perspective. Truth is relative to a context; context—perspective—is ignored only at the price of distortion. When we apply this device to the problem of immortality, we consider the occasion objectively immortal from the perspective of the ongoing world, and subjectively immortal from the perspective of God.

That an occasion can only be objectively immortal within finite successors follows from the nature of finite prehension. A finite occasion must prehend other occasions selectively, feeling the other from its own new standpoint and in accordance with the kind of harmony now made possible. The need for objectification stems from the conditions of creativity whereby the nascent occasion must narrow the creative possibilities offered by its past. The act of objectification lies in the partiality by which a becoming occasion prehends each past occasion. No finite occasion can prehend another occasion wholly; it must eliminate portions of each occasion through negative prehensions in order to unify its world through its own becoming. This selectivity of prehension violates the subjective unity of the prehended occasion, making it impossible for its own immediacy to be fully retained in the prehending occasion. "If you abolish the whole, you abolish its parts; and if you abolish any part, then *that* whole is abolished" (PR 288). There is indeed a reenactment of feelings from one occasion to the other; these conformal feelings may allow a high degree of sympathetic identity between occasions, but the identity is never complete—this would be impossible in finitude. The selectivity, even to the least degree, which operates in prehension disturbs the unity which, in its entirety, *is* the occasion. Therefore one occasion cannot reenact the full immediacy of any other; to the prehending occasion, the other is now objective. Selectivity of prehension destroys the subjective unity of the prehended occasion from the perspective of the prehending occasion. "We murder to dissect," spoke the poet Wordsworth, and the phrase aptly apples to finite prehension. The inclusion of the other is always a partial inclusion, and, therefore, always an objective inclusion. To one finite occasion another occasion is always objective.

If God, however, is able to prehend the entirety of an occasion's satisfaction—and Whitehead speaks of God as being without negative prehensions[16]—then the subjective unity of the occasion is not disturbed or divided in the prehension. It would be possible, then, for God to reenact the occasion wholly as a component in the divine nature, whereas the finite occasion can only reenact its predecessors partially. This would prepare the ground for positing that God, by feeling the wholeness of the prehended occasion, would feel its subjectivity as well.[17] In this case, the occasion would be subjectively immortal in God.

Whitehead gives grounds for considering this possibility in his enigmatic statements with reference to retention of immediacy for occasions in God.

In the temporal world, it is the empirical fact that process entails loss: the past is present under an abstraction. But there is no reason of any ultimate metaphysical generality why this should be the whole story (PR 340).

In [God's consequent nature] there is no loss, no obstruction. The world is felt in a unison of immediacy. The property of combining creative advance with the retention of mutual immediacy is what . . . is meant by the term 'everlasting' (PR 346).

In everlastingness, immediacy is reconciled with objective immortality (PR 351).

To explicate this further, consider the world in its relationship to God. Whitehead consistently conceives of the process of the world as a purposive movement toward the achievement of intensity of experience. This intensity is twofold. It is an intensity to be achieved within each finite occasion to the maximum degree possible within its standpoint, and it is an intensity within the very nature of God.

Within finite entities, the intensity of experience refers to the manner in which an occasion holds many possibilities, also called eternal objects, together in the actualized harmony of its own experience.[18] The greater the number of possibilities which the occasion can contrast and enjoy, the greater the intensity of its experience. The number of possibilities it can entertain is governed in part by what the entity has inherited from its past, and in part by its own perspectival capacity for novelty. Its subjective aim is to maximize the greatest degree of intensity possible, given these strictures.

The absolute standard of intensity is the primordial nature of God, which in itself is neither great nor small because it is simply the vision and valuation of all possibilities whatsoever.[19] Unlike the occasion, which requires a determining thrust from its past world toward its own new selection of possibilities, and hence an exclusive embodiment of relatively few possibilities, God's primordial vision is all-inclusive. All potentialities are known and valued by God; this inclusive vision is then the standard of relevance and intensity for the limited realization of possibilities within the actual occasions.

However, if God is already the holding together of all the eternal objects in such a way that God is the standard of intensity, what difference does the occasion's small achievement make to God? And if God's primordial nature is "neither great nor small," what sense does it make to speak of God's own aim toward an intensification of the divine immediacy?

The occasion's value to God cannot consist only in its togetherness of eternal objects, important though this is. Such togetherness has been known and valued by God eternally in the primordial vision. Rather, the peculiar contribution of the occasion is its vividness of actual embodiment of just those possibilities which it selects to the exclusion of all others. Its intensity of attainment is its valuation in the immediacy of itself. This alone can be the contribution of the occasion to God, but this is everything.

Consider the peculiar uniqueness of the occasion relative to God's primordial vision. The occasion is an utterly unique valuation in the decisiveness of its becoming, and hence quite different from the potentiality of the primordial vision. In the primordial vision, the value which has been attained by the entity was one possible value among many, and formed part of an inclusive pattern of potentiality. God's own valuation was not a negative cutting off of the potentialities, but a qualitative determination as to God's own manner of envisaging many values. Thus the potentiality in the vision of God is marked by an inclusiveness within an ultimate vision.

Not so for the occasion, however, for within its actuality its own valuation is quite exclusive. The occasion has valued just *this* togetherness of objects with its very being, cutting off all alternatives in the decisiveness of this one attainment. There is a sharpness of experience in its selectivity which must be lacking completely in the inclusive potentiality of the primordial vision. This discrete and concrete value, this vividness, this intensity which is its own immediacy, becomes its gift to God. And it is a peculiar realization of value which only a finite occasion can provide.

The immediacy of an occasion contributes to God's own intensification of experience by providing the contrasting sharpness of actuality to the potentiality of the primordial vision. Whereas the occasion experiences intensity through the contrasting eternal objects which it can hold together in its satisfaction, God experiences intensity through the contrasting actualities which can be held together as manifestations of the primordial vision, or satisfaction. Through the most extreme form of its actuality, the vividness of its satisfaction, the world is the instrument of novelty for God, even as through God's own form of potentiality God is the instrument of novelty for the world. God and the world, as contrasting opposites, each contribute to the intensity of immediacy of the other: God through potentiality, the world through actuality; God through the inclusiveness of the primordial vision, the world through the exclusiveness of the decisive satisfaction.

When intensities are understood as the maximal togetherness of embodied eternal objects, the dynamics by which these objects are held together—the subjective experience of the actual occasion—is of paramount importance. Not the remembrance of accomplished intensities but the presentness of experienced intensity is indicated as the continuous aim of God in the creative advance. The subjectivity of the occasion itself is of prime importance; the retention of this subjective immediacy in the everlasting presentness of God would then be the maximum fulfillment of God's purpose. Therefore, we hold that this very subjectivity is everlastingly retained in God's own consequent nature, and that it is this factor which leads Whitehead to the intuition of a final reconciliation of immediacy with objective immortality in everlastingness.

Whitehead himself did not understand objective immortality to be a function of the present in its requirements; on the contrary, he usually speaks of objective immortality in terms of the termination of an occasion. An occasion concresces, attains its unity of satisfaction, and becomes objectively immortal. By modifying him on this point, however, we clarify his many passages concerning the retention of an occasion's immediacy in God's own nature. An occasion concresces, enjoys its unity of satisfaction, and becomes superjectively immortal: objectively in finite occasions, and subjectively in God.

There are a number if implications which follow from placing the responsibility for objectification upon the prehending entity. The immediacy of an occasion culminates in satisfaction, or the internal completion of concrescence. From the perspective of the world, this internal completion marks the end of the occasion's immediacy, and its transition to the creative advance. But this advance is related to the continual call of God to the world toward process through the evocation of immediacies. Could it not be that this creative advance into new immediacy is made possible by the passage of the attained immediacy not into nothingness, nor into sheer memory, nor yet into the shrouded past, but into God? As God prehends the immediacy of the occasion, lifting it into the divine nature, is not this the making way for a new immediacy?

Subjective immediacy creates the frame of the present, but it does not persist—and if it did, the world would be statically filled and dead. Rather, there is a constant movement of immediacy surpassed by immediacy. Whitehead describes the movement from the perspective of the new future, and he simply recounts the dynamics which must occur given the process of the world. And the dynamics declare a movement from many to one to many again, a process that within the entity itself begins, becomes, and terminates. If indeed there is "no reason of any ultimate metaphysical generality why (loss) should be the whole story" (PR 340), if "in everlastingness immediacy is reconciled with objective immortality" (PR 351), then perhaps the passage of immediacy is merely our apprehension of the prehension of immediacy by God. The universe, in process thought, is a receiving and a giving: the occasion, having come to be, might enter this giving phase objectively for the world, according to the needs of that world, but subjectively for God, according to the needs of God.

Having said this, a major qualification must be made. If the way an entity prehends the past—objectively or subjectively—depends primarily upon the needs of the prehending entity and the consequent ability or inability of the entity to prehend other occasions in their entirety, then "objectivity" refers simply to a mode of prehension, to be distinguished from another and fuller mode of prehension, which retains subjectivity. As such, there is a basic compatibility between the two modes, and between objectivity and subjectivity per se. They are not as radically disjunctive as at first appears.

Indeed, it could well be the case that each implies the other. An occasion must prehend the past, and the past has achieved a particular satisfaction which determines a limitation on the number of ways in which the occasion may be objectified. But is it not so that when the present feels the past, it does so with some feeling of how the past felt itself? Although the primary mode of prehension is objective, there clings to this objectivity the sense of immediacy which prevailed for the predecessor. Here the vectoral notion of prehensions which Whitehead developed indicates a clothing of subjectivity within the very objectivity of the prehension. Although one occasion reenacts only a portion of the satisfaction which its predecessor felt, negatively prehending the remainder, these negative prehensions still have an effect. They qualify the subjective form which is reenacted with the intuition of what that form was in the context of its original immediacy; the new occasion reenacts and thus feels the feeling with some sense of how that feeling was felt by the predecessor—the preceding immediacy is implied. Thus while objectivity dominates, it does so with a feeling for the original subjectivity of its datum. This initial subjectivity cannot be reenacted completely, else there would be no new finite occasion, but it can be "understood." Thus the objective prehension of one occasion by another implies a conveyed sense of subjectivity as well.

It would be likewise in the case of God. Though God may prehend the subjective immediacy of the occasion, there is also the sense in which God knows that occasion in terms of its objectivity for others. The divine prehension of the occasion finally must include some objectivity if it is to be retained in full subjectivity, for in *Adventures of Ideas* Whitehead notes that the occasion feels its own future, which is to say, its objectivity for others.[20] Also, of course, each occasion contains its objectification of its own past. Hence for God to prehend the subjectivity of the occasion is to prehend as well its objectivity for the future, and the objectivity of its past. A difference of degree rather than kind obtains in whichever mode of prehension develops, for each mode indicates and to a degree includes the other.

If our suggestions are possible, then there is no reason within the occasion itself which would forbid a prehension that reenacts the full immediacy of the occasion, as enjoyed in the satisfaction. This reenactment of immediacy is not simply a duplication of immediacy; it would have to be a rebirth of the self-same immediacy. Given the circumstance in which an occasion is prehended with absolutely no negative prehensions and hence with no perspectival elimination, there is no violation of the subjective unity of the occasion.[21] The occasion *is* just this unification, just this value, just this decision. Therefore a total reenactment of the entity must result in a rebirth of just this immediacy. The occasion is twice-born: first through its own self-creation, and second through God's total prehension of this self-creation. Its temporal birth is as fleeting as the concrescence that generated it; its divine birth, grounded in God's own concrescence, is as everlasting as God. The occasion is therefore reborn to subjective immortality.

VI

Finitude and Everlasting Redemption: Participation in God

Subjective immortality can be only the beginning of an answer to the evil that is called loss. Everlasting retention of an immediacy is not sufficient to constitute the overcoming of evil, and in fact could itself constitute a form of evil. In the case of pain, the immortal retention of pain would resemble Augustine's hell, and in the case of pleasure, its immortal retention formed the first circle of Dante's hell.[1] Subjective immortality can establish a basis for the overcoming of evil, but it is not in itself a suffcient answer to evil.[2]

In order to answer evil, we must be able to establish that the occasion which is subjectively immortal in God participates in the divine concrescence, so that God's transformation of the occasion in accordance with God's own aim is a transformation for the occasion as well as for God. The occasion in God must be itself and more than itself. The problem in Whiteheadian terms, of course, is the insistence that the satisfaction of any entity admits no addition. If we posit that a prehended satisfaction participates in its own transformation, have we not violated its very nature? How can the occasion be itself and more than itself in God?

We propose to address the problem through three fundamental steps. First, we shall explore the nature of a satisfaction's completion, noting the sense in which it includes an anticipation of the future. This will be discussed in relation to its finite future and in relation to its everlasting future in God. Second, we will discuss the relation of the satisfaction to its transitional creativity, and the relation of its transitional creativity to God's concrescence, or the linkage of the immediacy of the occasion with the immediacy of God. Third, we will apply the dynamics of concrescence to God in order to suggest the nature of the apotheosized satisfaction's experience of transformation. This last will deal with apotheosis as judgment and peace.

The satisfaction of an occasion is both complete and incomplete: Complete with respect to its own decision, but incomplete with respect to the decisions of others concerning itself.

Thus each actual entity, although complete so far as concerns its microscopic process, is yet incomplete by reason of its objective inclusion of the macroscopic process. It really experiences a future which must be actual, although the completed actualities of that future are undetermined. In this sense, each actual occasion experiences its own objective immortality (PR 215).

We have argued that the immediacy of an occasion is not confined to its concrescence, but extends as well to its satisfaction: the subjective unity of the entire occasion is both process and outcome. In satisfaction the occasion's enjoyment has a double dimension. It enjoys itself as a new value in the world, and as a fresh requirement for another's unification. The occasion's enjoyment of itself as requiring a future beyond itself is its generation of transitional creativity, evoking new becomings. The finite future that is generated will be in one sense the temporal completion of the past. Through its anticipation of this future, the satisfaction enjoys the sense of its own completion.

The completion of an occasion relative to its future is simply the way in which the future accounts for that occasion. The occasion is a value, significant for its own being. This value implies future becomings which will incorporate that value in some way. Indeed, the anticipation of this further influence has been formative for the occasion in its value creating process, giving a certain open-endedness to the occasion. The satisfaction awaits a confirmation from beyond itself, a valuing of the value which it is.

However, the nature of finitude necessarily gives many valuations to the one value. The new occasion, coming into being through the force not of one, but of many predecessors, must objectify those predecessors. There is no way in which the novel occasion can retain, and hence wholly affirm, the value of any one predecessor. It can only reenact a perspectival portion of each former value, and hence confirm it only partially. This implication of process has been discussed in Chapters IV and V: the past fades through perspectival elimination, providing a tragic aspect to perpetual perishing. In the case of wholly negative prehensions, the new occasion can negate the total value of the other—but not as if that value had never been, since even negative prehensions bear the trace of that which they negate. Whitehead illustrates the partiality involved in objectification in the following:

This subjective unity of (A's) concrescence introduces negative prehensions, so that D in the direct feeling is not felt in its formal completeness, but objectified with the elimination of such of its prehensions as are inconsistent with D felt through the mediation of B, and through the mediation of C (PR 226).

While in this passage Whitehead discusses the necessity of elimination due to the mediating occasions of B and C, the situation is similar for any prehension. The prehended occasion is one among many, and, therefore, can only be rendered compatible for a new unification through negative prehensions regarding a portion of the occasion's value. Since the satisfaction to be prehended is a diversity held together in unity, the successor occasion may well bypass the original emphasis of the occasion, selecting instead an aspect of the diversity which functioned subordinately. In any case, the objectification of a satisfaction in terms of partiality wrests the prehended value from its subjective unity and its immediacy, consigning the satisfaction to a state of objectivity and of being only partially confirmed on the level of finitude. If the occasion's completion depends upon its confirmation through the world, then the occasion can never be completed through the world. Furthermore, since its meaning can be partially confirmed in the richness of many perspectives, its completion is a process potentially as infinite as the world.

Finite completion, however, is not limited to repetitive affirmation of the occasion's value from beyond itself; completion also entails the sense in which the entity contributes to patterns of meaning that are more than itself. The entity participates in what Whitehead calls the creative advance of nature. The microscopic reality of the occasion's own unification of many into its satisfaction yields to a macroscopic reality wherein it is itself a component in a process more than any single entity can achieve. This mode of completion goes beyond simple affirmation, and implies a transformation. The simplest illustration of this in Whiteheadian terms would be the manner in which many entity's together form the structure of a cell; many cells contribute to a body supporting personal existence; many persons create communities, and communities create nations. In each case, there is a completion that involves far more than simple affirmation; it is a completion that through many components creates patterns of meaning and beauty not possible at the level of the finite occasion alone.

The satisfaction of any single occasion may be simple or complex, and incorporate notions of its further completion accordingly. At the simplest level, such as an occasion within an inorganic society, the anticipation of the future might be a feeling for its simple repetition, or affirmation through similarity. At high grades of complexity, such as an entity within the personal society that Whitehead calls the soul of a human being, the anticipation of the future includes affirmation and transformation, with the two modes interrelated. The richest affirmation of the occasion's worth may be precisely through the transformations that the occasion makes possible in successor occasions. To say that a satisfaction includes a sense of its completion through the future—or, in Whitehead's words, experiences its own objective immortality—is to imply that an occasion's initial completion is open-ended, necessarily leading beyond itself, in varying modes of intensity.

Given the nature of finitude, the occasion can know its further completion only by way of anticipation. Insofar as that further completion involves a larger pattern of meaning, only the successor occasions will know the achievement or loss of that larger pattern, and then they in their turn must depend on their own futures for the completion of whatever further patterns they might have envisioned. Existence is perpetual perishing at several levels: the satisfaction is a flickering attainment, generated by concrescence, and then gone; further, given the necessary selectivity of successors, the satisfaction's fullness can never again be repeated in temporal reality. Nor can any satisfaction feel completely the larger pattern of meaning to which it might contribute. Such is objective immortality.

If, as was argued in Chapter V, objective immortality is paralleled by subjective immortality in God, what effect would this have upon the occasion's completion? Whitehead gives some intimation in the following passage.

God is completed by the individual, fluent satisfactions of finite fact, and the temporal occasions are completed by their everlasting union with their transformed selves, purged into conformation with the eternal order which is the final absolute 'wisdom' (PR 347).

If finite completion involves both affirmation and transformation, the same appears to be true with regard to an occasion's infinite completion in God. God's reception of the occasion in its full immediacy is the ultimate completion of an occasion insofar as it requires an affirmation from beyond itself, and "conformation with the eternal order" would likewise be an ultimate transformation. But while an occasion might anticipate such completion, how could the occasion participate in it beyond its dim foreshadowing in satisfaction?

Even though God prehends the subjective occasion into everlasting concrescence, the retention of the occasion's immediacy in this concrescence does not necessarily imply any change to that immediacy. But if it does not, then there is the danger that whatever has been experienced in finitude as unmitigated evil will continue to be experienced in such a fashion through all eternity. Such an eschatological "heaven" might well be described as "hell," since it would amount to a freezing of all time into the multitudinous instances of satisfaction. Process would apply to God, but not to the occasion frozen into everlasting immediacy. Better that the immediacy were not retained, than that it be retained with no transformation.

Since the occasion's anticipatory feelings of the future allow a certain open-endedness to the occasion, we propose further exploration of these feelings in relation to transitional creativity, building upon the developments of Chapter V. Anticipatory feelings generate transitional creativity, and we have noted in some detail how transitional creativity evokes the becoming of a new present, the occasion's future. But how does the occasion's generation of transitional creativity work vis-à-vis God? It cannot be to evoke God's concrescence, since God's concrescence precedes the finite entity and is everlastingly established.

The satisfaction of the occasion is an enjoyment of its unified self, and this enjoyment is a form of creativity. As such, it embodies the results of the creativity of concrescence, and looks forward to the creativity of its successors. It is a momentary "Janus" with a double reference: concrescence and transition, memory and anticipation—a breathing space between past and future. Prehended into God, the anticipation which was its generation of its finite future meets the everlasting generation of God. Like tendrils finding root, the transitional creativity of the satisfaction grounds its immediacy within the divine concrescence. The satisfaction that was generated through its finite concrescence becomes sustained by the divine concrescence, whereby its anticipation meets its ultimate end.

Transitional creativity, then, becomes the mode whereby the occasion can become itself and more than itself in God. The occasion is linked into the concrescence of God, even while remaining itself. Thus the peculiarity obtains that the occasion is *both* itself *and* God: it is apotheosized.[3] As a participant in the divine concrescence, it will feel its own immediacy, and God's feeling of its immediacy as well. From God's perspective, God prehends the entity in its entire immediacy, incorporating it and therefore sustaining it within the divine concrescence. God's feeling of the divine self thereby necessarily includes a co-feeling of the entity's feelings of itself. From the entity's perspective, its transitional creativity, generated through its anticipatory feelings, meets God's concrescent creativity and is conjoined with that creativity, even while still being generated by the now everlastingly sustained finite satisfaction. The entity enjoys its own satisfaction *and* God's consciousness of it, in the unity of God's now extremely complex subjectivity.

In the apotheosis, the finite satisfaction remains itself even while it experiences God's transforming power. How is it that the continuing experience does not alter the satisfaction? Does the analysis of the entity as a bit of becoming which, once become, is evermore that one thing, break down in the further understanding of an apotheosis of the world? It might seem as if each prehended immediacy, by being united with the totality of God, must then become as a series in its continued experience of God. This would entail that every occasion, no matter whence its organic origination, is ultimately destined for a continual seriality in everlastingness.[4] But this would undercut again the occasion's own participation in the redemption available to it in God. It must be the same occasion which is retained in God which is then redeemed through God; successor occasions cannot fulfill this basic requirement of redemption.

The way to approach the problem lies in the distinction between the genetic time of concrescence, and the serial time marked by transition. What we call time is our marking of the successiveness of occasions. But the internal process of concrescence is not properly called time at all, for while there is a processive refinement of data, this does not involve loss. Each datum is retained *and* modified as the concrescent process takes place, for the datum is contrasted in relation to other data, and integrated accordingly into the satisfaction. The datum is thus itself and more than itself in relation to the whole. Only temporally, in the seriality of successive occasions, does the loss of time obtain.

If we apply this to God, the only difference is the retention of the occasion's felt immediacy in satisfaction, conjoined now with God's own immediacy through God's self-defined subjective aim. It is as if the edges of God receive the satisfaction, which then relates to the divine concrescence through transitional creativity. Whereas in the objective prehensions of finite relation transitional creativity breaks with the intitial entity to become the sole concrescent energy of the new occasion, in the divine relation this break does not happen. Transitional creativity acts instead as a linkage between the immediacy of the occasion and the immediacy of God. In entities which include consciousness, there is a dual consciousness: the retained consciousness of the satisfaction, and the moving consciousness of God. Thus in apotheosis the occasion experiences itself and more than itself, which is to say, the occasion experiences itself and God's evaluative transformation of itself within the divine nature.

The occasion's experience in God is governed by God's own subjective aim. God is an entity, prehending others into a unity through God's own concrescent principle of unification—that aim toward beauty, harmony, and peace which Whitehead discusses in the closing chapters of *Adventures of Ideas*. In the divine concrescence, the many values of the occasions are compared and contrasted with each other and with God's own aim, analogously to the concrescence of any reality. This requires that God feel each value for its own sake and for the sake of all others as well. Through this contrasting, the occasions become a diverse unity manifesting the divine satisfaction, much as each occasion's own satisfaction is a diversity held into the unity of its decision. The unity of God, retaining the immediacy of each prehended occasion, is community, an ultimate and transforming togetherness which confirms and redeems finite reality.

God's creation of harmony from the vast diversity of the individual immediacies follows from the fourth mode of dealing with diverse and/or conflicting values within concrescence as given by Whitehead in *Adventures of Ideas*.[5] There Whitehead considers several ways of achieving harmony despite discordance: through negative prehensions of the potential disruption, so that it is simply blocked from effect; through utter conformity to the potentially disruptive prehension, which then entails the negative prehension of the quieter weight of inherited influence; and thirdly, through the reduction of the discordancies to a background through lessening the intensities of discordant elements to a least common multiple factor. Again, this third alternative, like the other two, involves negative prehensions, and so is excluded from God's mode of harmonizing the universe, since God is without negative prehensions. There is then a higher way of harmony:

This fourth way is by spontaneity of the occasion so directing its mental functions as to introduce a third system of prehensions, relevant to both the inharmonious systems. This novel system is such as radically to alter the distribution of intensities throughout the two given systems, and to change the importance of both in the final intensive experience of the occasion (*AI* 260).

In God this "third system of prehensions" would simply be the principle of unification, or God's subjective aim toward harmony— that "overpowering rationality of conceptual harmonization" (*PR* 346). Given this overwhelming thrust toward harmony in a nature which is transpersonal since it incorporates many immediacies, values which were formerly mutually obstructive would now assume the importance of contrasts, each highlighting the other relative to God's own aim. An inclusive harmony reduces competitiveness to complementation. There is no vying for one value at the expense of another, since both co-exist in the harmonious immediacy of God, where each is affirmed for what it is. Hence, the uniqueness is magnified rather than threatened; contrasting values benefit from each other since each underscores the uniqueness of the other. Thus the exclusive valuations formed in finitude find complementation in the inclusiveness of the infinitely expanding consequent nature of God. In such a situation, the meaning of each is not destroyed or substantially changed by otherness, but is intensified, deepened. Each meaning receives importance again and again as it is contrasted and complemented by every other immediacy within the diverse unity of God. Even those occasions which on the finite level would be a threat to each other's continued influence are, in God, a completion of each other through their mutual reinforcement of the unique meaning of each. Insofar as each finite occasion is linked into God's consciousness of these contrasts, each occasion experiences itself from God's perspective. In so doing, the anticipatory feelings of finitude meet their infinite completion.

Meanwhile, if contrasting values enhance each other within the inclusive harmonization being actualized in God, how much more so do those values which are inherently compatible. The openness of each immediacy to its own completion is also an openness to the completion of others; reciprocity obtains in the nature of God, since all share in the unification of God: an occasion completes as it is completed in the everlasting concrescence. Within such a process of completion, an immediacy feels its relationship with all others, compatible and incompatible, but finds its meaning particularly deepened in essentially compatible values. Here the benefit which each gives to the other stems not from an external contrast, but from an internal affirmation: within each occasion's integral being there is that which touches another in basic kinship. Yet the richness of such mutual affirmation stems again from the distinctiveness of each entity: the values are not identical, but essentially compatible. The differences enhance the compatibility, much as a variety of perspectives on a single theme enriches, deepens, and intensifies that theme. Even so, the sameness-in-difference of compatible values confers an inexhaustible beauty on the value thus shared and affirmed; this beauty is felt by the occasions insofar as it is felt by God, so that the occasions are truly the end and not simply the means of God's purpose.

The harmony of each finite satisfaction as it completes another finite satisfaction through intensification of meaning, whether through contrast or similarity, takes place through God's mutuality of subjective form, or God's own feeling of how each of the occasions taken into the divine nature relates to all of the others. The infinite giving and receiving which is the harmony of the harmonies occurs as each occasion, related to the primordial vision through the subjective form with which it is felt, feels its own relationship through God to all others.

This depiction of God is as both eternal and everlasting: eternal in the one aim derived from the primordial nature toward a vision of Peace, including harmony, zest, and beauty; and everlasting in the concrete manifestation of this aim through the occasions of the world as they are prehended into the divine nature. Every aspect of God's concrescence is a moving manifestation of God's primordial vision, and a realization of God's subjective aim. Insofar as God's own immediacy incorporates the many immediacies of the prehended world, God is the Immediacy of immediacies, and a Harmony of harmonies. Each prehended immediacy must retain its identity in order to contribute to the harmony, but by the same token, its identity opens into the larger identity which is God. The One in many, and the many in One—"the many absorbed everlastingly in the final unity" (PR 347)—this is the nature of God. By being taken into this nature, the immediacy which has formed itself in finitude becomes a factor in infinitude, and therefore participates in the everlasting presentness of the divine life.

The retained immediacy, held in being by the divine concrescence, is rooted in that fuller Immediacy and grafted into the divine consciousness. Its own being becomes a participant in God's becoming, yielding the "more" of transformation which is God's feeling of the occasion's contribution to the total pattern. The occasion is "saved by its relation to the completed whole" (PR 346). The immediacy of the occasion is then both itself and others, both one and many, both finite and infinite in the ultimate togetherness which is God.

The occasion's participation in God is its experience of judgment. The contrasting and comparing that takes place through the divine concrescence is felt not simply as a whole, but as it affects each part. Given the multiple consciousness in God—the Immediacy containing many immediacies—the comparison relative to each part is judgmental, and this is necessary for the fullness of transformation. The judgment is multiple: it is a judgment of the occasion as it could have been relative to what it in fact became; it is a judgment of the occasion as a single satisfaction in relation to the communities in which it participated, such as the totality of a living person; it is a judgment of the occasion and, if applicable, its personhood, in relation to the increasingly wider communities of the whole universe; and it is throughout, of course, a judgment of the occasion in relation to God.

The first experience of judgment follows simply from God's reception of the occasion. After all, the initial aim for its best mode of becoming was God-given; its prehension of God was its access to God's own hopes for how it might creatively unify the objective data of its own past. In the freedom of its own concrescence, it responded to God's aim, whether by adoption or adaptation. God's prehension of the resultant satisfaction is not simply God's reception of a novel actuality, but God's reception of an anticipated actuality. The finite satisfaction is the fulfillment of God's anticipation relative to this particular occasion. Therefore, God's first experience through pre-hension of the satisfaction would be the evaluative knowledge of what the occasion became relative to what it could have become. The occasion, grafted into God, would feel again its initial aim in all the clarity of God's own nature, and feel as well itself as measured against that aim. Inasmuch as concrescent feelings are evaluative, with joy or with sorrow, the occasion experiences its judgment from God's perspective, feeling fully the divine responsiveness to its being.

Concrescence, however, is not simply the feeling of a single pre-hension, but the feeling of many held together in contrast. We earlier spoke of the occasion's participation in wider communities of kin-ship; the closest, of course, for occasions of immediate interest to us, is the community of presonhood to which each occasion directly contributes. How is there a judgment of persons? To answer this, we must first note the radical transcendence of personality involved, and make a brief discursion into the meaning of personhood in this system.

We are discussing a metaphysics whereby occasions of experience, not substantial persons, are resurrected into the life of God. Persons are composed of a whole society of actual occasions continuously coming into being and perishing. The soul is envisioned by Whitehead as that stream of occasions, formed primarily by the dominance of the mental pole, which provides the organizing center of this particular bodily society and hence the creation of personality. One might say that the consciousness of personhood achieves its unity in that each concrescent immediacy includes reflective consciousness not of its own experience, but of the experience of its immediate predecessor.[6] It prehends the consciousness of its past, and creates a consciousness for its immediate future. The sense of continuity, in this extension of Whitehead, is thus normally the defining characteristic of person-ality. But the metaphysical reality is that the person is composed of discrete occasions, and each occasion is prehended by God upon its completion. There can be no holding off of this divine prehension until the person herself or himself perishes. Thus the person in finite existence is a movement from one dominant occasion to the next, in seriality, whereas the person reborn moment by moment into God is the togetherness of all occasions which are or have been the whole person's life, body and soul. The stress is on the rebirth of each occasion, not the person—although, of course, to contain all the occasions that have ever formed a person is to resurrect that person in a far fuller sense than would ever be possible in the seriality of time.

One could say that occasions are resurrected directly, and persons indirectly insofar as the particular togetherness of occasions created just this person. This would mean, then, that in God *all* events or times of a person are present, and not simply the final event in the total series of the soul. In God, finite personal identity is "thick," much deeper than the "thinness" of seriality. The wholeness of a person's life is present, and not simply the concluding moment. One could envisage then a multiple transcendence of personality in God: first a transcendence of seriality into the fullness of the self; second, a transcendence of selfhood through the mutuality of feeling with all other selves and occasions, and third and most deeply, a transcendence of selves into the Selfhood of God. The concrescent subjectivity of God is the unifying force whereby the occasions formerly held in seriality are again created as a composite personality in God.

To return now to the sense of judgment relative to an occasion, if its first experience of judgment is the immediate sense of God's valuation of its becoming, its second sense of judgment follows from God's contrasting it with all the previously prehended occasions of a person's life. God's knowledge of this occasion relative to its whole personal past is the occasion's knowledge as well: insofar as this involves the fulfillment or disappointment of hopes, it is a judgment. If the person's temporal life continues, it is a judgment with anticipation of further knowledge regarding the whole of one's life. As in the judgment of the occasion itself vis-à-vis God's anticipatory hopes for it, the knowledge of oneself in relation to one's whole personhood is accompanied with the joy or sorrow of God's own valuation.

The contrasting of occasions in God does not stop with those of immediate kinship, but extends to increasing widths of community. Insofar as God's mutuality of subjective form feels each occasion in relation to others, each occasion feels the experiences of all others relative to itself: it experiences the pain or blessing it has caused, the hurts and the joys. It knows experientially each destruction it has inflicted, and this is judgment. Since this knowledge is mediated through God's mutuality of subjective form, it incorporates God's divine response to the situation: if God pains to feel the world's pain, the occasion feels that pain as well; if there is divine wrath at finite destruction, the occasion feels that as well.

Since concrescence is a comparing and contrasting of every pre-hended item with every other prehended item, the judgment encountered in the divine nature is as wide as one's influence in the ever-expanding universe—and in a process universe, everything affects everything else. Knowledge is judgment, a complete and utterly true sense of one's own contextual value. "The sense of worth beyond itself is immediately enjoyed as an overpowering element in the individual self-attainment" (*PR* 350). This sense of worth, whether for good or for ill, is the everlasting self-judgment and divine judgment upon the occasion.[7]

And yet, while such a judgment might in temporal circumstances create a weight of sorrow because of the evil the occasion might have entailed, in God this cannot be so—the judgment must also be peace. The inexorable corollary to the relation to the whole is not only the final availability of a clear judgment of one's worth, but the compan-ion fact of one's own integral relation to a whole that surpasses personality. The very unity of God's being, the oneness which is the ground of the unified multiplicity, means that the value of the whole rebounds to the subjectivity of each part. No occasion, however adverse its sense of its own worth may be, is excluded from the harmony of the whole. The whole has come into being just as much through this attainment as through all others. The whole is no abstract being, but the togetherness of all occasions in the unity of a harmony which is ever-intensifying through its ever-expanding nature. Just as the one contributes to the many, even so the many contribute to the one; the harmony finally belongs to every partici-pant. Thus no occasion is locked into its own small achievement. In the transcendence that belongs to it in God, it experiences a "con-formation of purpose to an ideal beyond personal limitations" (*AI* 291), and this conformation is its peace. The judgment that flows from the occasion's relation to the whole is finally, then, a knowledge of one's participation and belonging within the completed whole: judgment is transformation, redemption and peace.

In our focusing on the everlasting completion of the occasion in God, we have had to refer to the eternal aspect of its completion in relation to its union with God's subjective aim, derived from the primordial nature. We must expand on this, bringing out more fully the manner in which an occasion remains itself in God, and is yet transformed. We refer to the "transformed selves" which are "purged into conformation with the eternal order which is the final absolute 'wisdom' " (PR 347). The transformation of self, in union with God's aim, must be the manifestation of God's aim through the self's being in relation to the whole. But this manifestation of God's aim requires a participation in the primordial vision, and therefore the occasion's sense of its own inclusion in a harmony which transcends itself. Thus the essence of an occasion's union with God is its final bursting of the bonds of selfhood even while affirming that selfhood: the language is not paradoxical, for the reference is simply to a self, a value, which *is* in its givingness, its relatedness to a whole which by far transcends it.

Whitehead refers to such a glimpse of the now dynamic union with God's primordial character in terms of Peace:

It is hard to define, and difficult to speak of. It is not a hope for a future, nor is it an interest in present details. It is a broadening of feeling due to the emergence of some deep metaphysical insight, unverbalized and yet momentous in its coordination of values. Its first effect is the removal of the stress of acquisitive feeling arising from the soul's preoccupation with itself. Thus Peace carries with it a surpassing of personality.... Peace is the removal of inhibition and not its introduction. It results in a wider sweep of conscious interest. It enlarges the field of attention. Thus Peace is self-control at its widest,—at the width where the 'self' has been lost, and interest has been transferred to coordinations wider than personality (AI 285).

Peace ... is a harmony of the soul's activities with ideal aims that lie beyond any personal satisfaction (AI 288).

This union within the inclusiveness of the primordial vision as it is manifested in the consequent nature of God is thus both the ultimate confirmation and transcendence of the self. In terms of the occasion's immediacy, it is the affirmation of its decisive value, and the acknowledgment of its transitional effects as belonging essentially to all others. This transitional belonging is that self-transcendence, that mode of completion which is everlastingly mutual: that union of all occasions within the divine nature. This is the final, absolute wisdom, and the transformation of a self in the depth and width of peace.

The meaning of an occasion, then, is far wider than that which is initially formed in concrescence. Insofar as the occasion becomes related to the far-reaching effects of its meaning, it transcends itself, becoming related to all that is. And yet it is just itself which is so related: it is its own meaning, and no other, which is affirmed, contrasted, deepened, and judged through its transpersonal relations in the entire nature of God. The final completion of an occasion is its transformation in God through its relation to all others in the unifying concrescence of God, manifesting the primordial vision of God. This completion must be felt by the occasion itself, since its immediacy is retained in its satisfaction, and since this satisfaction is now grounded in God's own subjective concrescence through its transitional creativity and through God's subjective form.

The emphasis in this discussion has been upon the experience of the occasion in God as it senses its completion beyond itself. But there are two further points which must be made: first, the activity whereby the occasion experiences this completion is directed by God —it is God's subjectivity into which the occasion is now incorporated, and hence God's subjective aim and God's own freedom governs the process. The occasion is therefore not free to accept or reject its completion within God, for freedom belongs with the concrescing subject. This is now God. The occasion's freedom was exercised in its finite process of becoming, and was exhausted in that process. Hence its incorporation into God is an incorporation into the freedom of God. Insofar as the occasion's finite decision moved in conformity with God's own desires for it, then the occasion's experience of God's freedom would be experienced as an extension and fulfillment of its own freedom; insofar as its finite decision was contrary to God's purposes, the experience of God's freedom would be felt as the restriction of its own.

The second point to be made has to do with the unified consciousness of God in everlasting concrescence. We can speak of the immediacies within God, and therefore of God as the Immediacy of immediacies. Insofar as the finite immediacy involved consciousness, that consciousness is retained in God, but now as an aspect of God's own consciousness. God is conscious of feeling each prehension in terms of a mutuality of subjective form, which is to say that God feels each prehension within the consequent nature in terms of all other prehensions, with contrasts, intensifications, and judgment. Since it is God's concrescence sustaining the finite satisfaction within God, the finite satisfaction has become a participant in God, so that its finite consciousness is related to divine consciousness, and hence participates in the mutuality of subjective form whereby it is completed through the contrasts developed above. The concrescing contrasts are governed by God's subjective aim, flowing from God's primordial envisagement. Hence the movement of the finite occasion in God is a movement of integration with God's primordial vision.

To return to the discussion at the level of the occasion, as the occasion is woven into God's primordial vision it feels its everlasting manifestation of that vision. This applies to every occasion at whatever level of mentality that occasion has developed: it feels itself in the nature of God according to that value that it forged through its own becoming. Insofar as the occasion concerned embodied consciousness, then that consciousness continues in God, reflecting consciously its relation to the whole.

The immortality of the occasion in God is a participation in the "multiple unifications of the universe" (PR 349). Inasmuch as the consequent nature of God is everlastingly expanding, the whole to which the occasion relates is everlastingly changing; the meaning of the occasion derives new perspectives of enriching and of enrichment with every prehension of God. An occasion in God thus retains its own value, that which God has reenacted in bringing it again to birth, but experiences an ever-intensifying meaning to that value as it continuously feels its worth beyond itself. It is able to feel this worth, first of all, because the immediacy of its satisfaction relates to the transitional effects of this satisfaction, which is the completion of the entity, and second, because this completion is mediated to it through the concrescing activity of the everlasting nature of God.

Such a vision of the overcoming of evil relates to the cosmic harmony of classical thought and to the realization of the preestablished harmony of Leibniz. Infinity, meeting finitude, answers to the destruction and loss of meaning which obtains in temporality. Finitude, meeting infinity, gives definiteness and actuality to the otherwise amorphous values of infinity. The "universal pattern" of Whitehead's "Mathematics and the Good" is realized concretely in the everlasting nature of God.

Yet the marked difference of this version of a cosmic harmony from those developed by Augustine and Leibniz is the openness of the harmony to all values achieved in the universe whatsoever. Evil as well as good meets the transforming power of God. The consequent harmony is preestablished only in the sense that by the power and goodness and freedom of God all of the prehended immediacies *will* harmonize, but this is determined only in the barest metaphysical outlines. The values, the content which fleshes those outlines in actuality, depend upon the self-creativity of the universe. There is neither predestined essence nor predetermined utilization of freedom; rather, there is an openness toward a novel future where whatsoever values are actualized in the freedom of finite creativity are taken into the divine harmony. History determines the notes of the harmony; God determines their order and arrangement. Nor is there a preestablished conclusion to the harmony, wherein the universe comes to an end of history. Worlds indeed may come to an end, and even more so the civilizations within them, but no such end can or need be seen with regard to finitude per se. There is an open future, and a freedom for the future continuously operating in the present.

The fundamental difference from an Augustinian vision, of course, is the universal redemption required in this particular eschatology.[8] The universality of redemption is required since finitude as well as freedom is implicated as the source of evil. However, like Augustine's vision, the development given here entails a judgment which indicates an everlasting consequence to the evils which one freely incurs in this life. But for Augustine, the judgment was a final judgment in an eternal damnation; here the judgment is a transformation which moves from the experiential knowledge of one's effects to the inexorably required and purgative participation in God's own life. Whitehead's vision involves an "apotheosis of the world" (PR 348) which is its salvation.

Among the eschatologies considered earlier, only Augustine and Leibniz gave sustained attention to the nature of existence beyond history. Nietzsche, however, did posit an "eternal return" of all the universe. Interestingly, if subjective immortality is attained in God without any possibility of the finite subject experiencing the effects of that immortality, then the vision would not be unlike Nietzsche's eternal return. The existential effect of eternal recurrence for Nietzsche was the insistent affirmation of history in all its stubborn givenness, whether trivial or great, agonizing or ecstatic; it was the "yes" to one's own and all existence. The retention of the self-same immediacy in everlastingness is akin to such an affirmation, but the identification of that everlastingness as God, and the subsequent transformation of meaning, constitutes a significant change from the Nietzschean vision. However, this development, like his, requires a strong affirmation of history.

We claimed that history determines the notes of the divine harmony, but it is also the case that the harmony influences history. The relation is always reciprocal, so that "the perfected actuality passes back into the temporal world, and qualifies this world so that each temporal actuality includes it as an immediate fact of relevant experience" (PR 351). Thus the redemption of an occasion in God becomes a factor in the temporal redemption that occurs in the world; this redemption is mediated through the initial aim of God. We turn now to this discussion of the temporal overcoming of evil.

VII

Freedom and Temporal Redemption:
The Historical Community

How does everlasting redemption relate to the ongoing world? What is the structure of temporal redemption? We will attempt to answer these questions through a discussion of the unity of the primordial and consequent natures in God, whereby both are necessarily involved in God's creative action toward the world. This will prepare the way for a discussion of freedom and redemption in the world, whereby evil may be overcome at least in part.

We have spoken in some detail about the "phase of perfected actuality, in which the many are one everlastingly, without the qualification of any loss either of individual identity or of completness of unity" (PR 350-51). Whitehead refers to this as a third phase of actuality, following upon the phases of conceptual and physical origination, or the primordial nature of God and the multiplicity of actualities in the world. The third phase is the completion of the first two, and yet it is not an end to process. Rather, it leads to a fourth phase, which is the continuous infusion of the highest ideals of harmony into the world.

The action of the fourth phase is the love of God for the world. It is the particular providence for particular occasions. What is done in the world is transformed into a reality in heaven, and the reality in heaven passes back into the world. By reason of this reciprocal relation, the love in the world passes into the love in heaven, and floods back again into the world (PR 351).

115

Clearly, the overcoming of evil which takes place in the everlasting redemption of occasions within God has an effect in the ongoing world. It places a demand upon that world that it reflect the divine image in modes which God makes available to it. The redemption in heaven demands its likeness on earth. This demand comes to the world through the initial aim which God offers to each concrescing occasion.[1]

Whitehead has suggested at the beginning of Process and Reality that both the primordial and consequent natures of God are involved in the initial aim, but he gives little explicit attention to the role of the consequent nature.[2] However, it would appear that the reality of the world as felt through the consequent nature establishes the relevance of the possibilities from the primordial vision to the ongoing world. Further, the reality of the overcoming of evil in God is the ground of the hope that specific evils, whose effects continue destructively in the temporal world, may also be overcome temporally. This everlasting and divine overcoming of evil provides the specific paths which can lead to temporal redemption. Temporal redemption rests upon everlasting redemption, and is mediated to the concrescing occasions of the world through the initial aim which each occasion receives from God. The actualization of this redemption depends upon the freedom of the world.

Throughout *Process and Reality* Whitehead has emphasized the importance of the primordial nature of God as it relates to the initial aim of the occasion and, macrocosmically, as it relates to the creative advance of nature as a whole. Because God is that nontemporal actuality whose "origination" stems from the mental conception of eternal possibilities, there is novelty and order in the universe rather than chaos or sheer repetition. Whitehead portrays this propulsion toward order in the world as being directly due to the primordial nature of God.

This initial phase [for the actual occasion] is a direct derivate from God's primordial nature. In this function, as in every other, God is the organ of novelty, aiming at intensification (PR 67).

But the initial stage of its [the actual occasion's] aim is an endowment which the subject inherits from the inevitable ordering of things, conceptually realized in the nature of God. . . . Thus the transition of creativity from an actual world to the correlate novel concrescence is conditioned by the relevance of God's all-embracing conceptual valuations to the particular possibilities of transmission from the actual world (PR 244).

The differentiated relevance of eternal objects to each instance of the creative process requires their conceptual realization in the primordial nature of God (PR 257).

These passages give no indication of the importance of the conse-qent nature to the initial aim, and these passages are fair samples of the majority of Whitehead's statements on the subject.[3] Thus White-head leaves to his followers the task of demonstrating the role of the consequent nature in the provision of initial aims.

The major support for such a task is the necessary unity of God. While Whitehead speaks easily in terms of a primordial nature and a consequent nature, he no more intends an acutal division in the reality of God than he does in any other entity—God is not an exception to metaphysical principles. Only in the abstraction of analysis can the primordial and consequent natures be treated in separation—and Whitehead does indeed call such a separation a "distinction of reason" (PR 344). However, Whitehead overwhelm-ingly makes this distinction of reason, treating the two natures rather separately. Therefore, in this and in our final chapter we will focus upon the unity of God, demonstrating that only in integration is either the primordial or consequent nature effective. The effect of this integration with respect to the ongoing world provides the means of redemption.

The primordial nature of God is the permanent conceptualization of all possibilities, together with their ordering in terms of value. But the valuation is not simply an arrangement of possibilities and possibilities of possibilities in hierarchies of various worlds, culmin-ated by a vision of the best possible world for all times and places, with an aim toward its creation. If this were the case, then appetition toward actuality would result in the temporal unfolding of the eternal vision, entailing a contradiction of freedom similar to that which appeared in Leibniz. That such does not happen in a Whiteheadian view is entailed by the qualitative rather than quantitative character of the vision, and by its continual dynamism through integration with the consequent nature. This precludes a fixed "best," and avoids the Leibnitian dilemma.

What, then, is the character of God's valuation of possibilities in the primordial evisagement? While Whitehead alludes to the primordial valuation in *Process and Reality* in terms of the urge toward intensity of experience, it is not until he writes *Adventures of*

Ideas that he more fully expounds the character of such intensity.[4] In this book, intensity as a value is not simply the complex holding of a diversity in unity, as is suggested in *Process and Reality*, but is qualitatively described as adventure, zest, truth, beauty, and peace. It is not that God is envisioned as having five separable valuations; rather, the evaluative vision of God is a complex unity, where possibilities are so ordered that their way of combining is the intensity which is itself a manifestation of adventure, zest, truth, beauty, and peace. Thus the vision is as much a matter of *how* the possibilities are held together as it is what is held together. The reality is so ordered that it manifests the five qualities in reciprocal enrichment, so that Whitehead can refer to the whole vision of God with the notion of Harmony. In order actually to be harmony, however, it is necessary that it apply not simply to possibilities but to actuality. Thus the vision of harmony carries an appetition toward actuality for its fulfillment.[5]

There is an essential openness to the primordial envisagement which requires the actuality of a finite world for its realization. Since the consequent nature is God's feeling of the world, the consequent nature is essential for actualization of the primordial vision within the life of God.[6] The integration of the natures is essential.

While Whitehead names these natures as primordial and consequent in God, they are analogous to the finite entity's mental and physical poles. The unity of the two poles in every entity, whether God or a finite occasion, is a dynamic process of concrescence that unifies the data of the physical pole through the vision of the mental pole. We hold until our final chapter a detailed argument for a "reversed concrescence" in God due to the reversal of the divine polar structure, which marks the satisfaction of God as primordial and dynamic. It is sufficient for the work of this chapter and the Leibnitian question posed above to demonstrate that the unity of God requires a relativization of God's qualitative vision with respect to the world, and hence an openness and transforming adaptability to any world.

The consequent nature of God is continuously incorporating the world into the divine nature; this incorporation, as discussed in our former chapters, involves the full immediacy of the occasion. But if God is considered an actual entity, one can hardly imagine the prehended world simply sitting at the edges of God. Rather, the world must be pulled into the concrescence of God, which is governed by God's subjective aim for actualization of the primordial vision. The actualization of the vision happens first and foremost in God, through just these prehended occasions. The vision qua vision is abstract, sheerly possible. God to be God must be more than vision; God must be the actuality of that vision. This actualization, however, can only be attained through the concrescence of God, and the concrescence relates to a very specific world which has been pre-hended. It is precisely this world which the transforming concrescent power of God must render into a manifestation of the primordial vision. Thus the actualization of the vision even within God is relativized. The abstract harmony of all possibilities becomes a concrete harmony of just these living actualities within God. The reality of zest, adventure, truth, beauty, and peace is an ever-changing kaleidoscopic reorganization of the primordial vision in accordance with the way in which any particular world may be transformed.[7]

In comparison to Leibniz, then, Whitehead's vision offers not the best of all possible worlds, but the best possible for any world. God's subjective aim toward the realization of possibilities is clothed with the feeling for harmony, implying or containing within that feeling the intent toward adventure, zest, truth, beauty, and peace: qualitative feelings which can be manifested in an infinite variety of ways. The Whiteheadian valuation in its qualitative sense refers not to a previsioned world, but to qualities which would work to the ultimate enhancement of *any* world. No world is considered in every minute detail, compared to others, and judged comparatively as best; rather, a quality of existence is envisioned which can be infinitely applied to an infinite number of worlds, clothing them all with that which is best given their own particular variations of actuality. The notion of successive worlds is important, because a "best of all possible worlds" could theoretically be achieved in time, and then the aim as aim would be exhausted. In Whitehead's vision, the aim is infinitely achievable, and infinitely achieved precisely because it is qualitative rather then quantitative.

If the primordial vision is being relativized within the actuality of God, how does this affect the continuing creation of the world? The occasions being transformed within the activity of God are also those that are being objectively prehended in the temporal world by their finite successors. For good or for ill, they have each and all together delimited the boundaries of real potentiality for these successors. Further, it belongs to the nature of the process that each occasion's influence is determined by what it is; there is a demand for repetition of its own value. In more complex occasions, the demand for repetition can be combined with a thrust toward transformation through some larger system of meaning. The successor occasion, however, is affected not by any single occasion alone, but by a great multiplicity of occasions, each demanding its influence. Thus if we consider the phenomenon of a new unification simply on the basis of the transitional creativity of the immediate past, we are faced with a conundrum. There is an essential competitiveness to the past. If each satisfaction generates a transitional creativity which is a demand for its own peculiar influence, and this is multiplied a thousandfold, then how does this multitude of transitional creativities do anything other than cancel each other out? The burden of unifying this insistent stream of competing energies would seem staggering if not paralyzing. Chaos, not order, would reign if the world were left to itself.

However, the creative power of God is such that God alone, through the resources of the primordial envisagement, can prehend the entirety of these competing energies. Because God is already the unification of all possibility, there is in principle no actuality which is incompatible with the divine nature, and no actuality which is incapable of transformation into the divine harmony.[8] This transformation proceeds in stages. The initial prehension by God and into God takes place upon an occasion's completion.[9] The effect of this prehension is that God's reality is informed by the internal feeling of the togetherness of as many occasions as have become actual in the world.

Furthermore, God's feeling of these occasions is through the "mutuality of subjective form," which means that these completed occasions are felt relative to one another, and relative to God's own aim toward harmony.[10] The effect of this is that while in the world the many are indeed a clamoring many, each demanding its own due, the counterpart of that very world in God is a beginning toward unification in terms of God's own particular aim toward harmony. God's initial feeling of mutuality whereby each occasion is related to all others, directed by the resources of the primordial envisagement, is of immediate relevance to the finite prehenders of these occasions. God's transformation of the occasion suggests parallel modes of transformation in the becoming world, so that new possibilities move into relevance for that world, and are incorporated into God's moving satisfaction as anticipatory feelings for the world. Like a great intensity of light striking a prism and breaking into many colors, the harmony in God is reflected to myriad standpoints in the nascent world as so many definite possibilities for modes of mutual relating in the world which is about to be. The initial mode of the redemption which occurs in God provides the possibilities for redemption in the world. The progressive concrescence of God, of course, provides the continuing adventure wherein the fullness of transformation accomplishes the joy of the primordial vision relative to this prehended world. But it is the initial stages of redemption in God which account for the movement of primordial possibilities into real rather than merely potential relevance for the world.

The initial aim which each occasion receives from God is not unlike the aims received from all other entities, save for its content. The novel aspect of God's satisfaction relative to the becoming entity is that God's unification of the same past which the nascent occasion prehends has been accomplished through the resources of the infinite possibilities of the primordial vision. God's satisfaction, relative to the occasion, contains more than any one of the satisfactions given in the occasions of the past and more than all the occasions in the past taken together. The novel ingredient in God's satisfaction relative to the new occasion is an optimum way for *how* a new finite unification can be accomplished from as many standpoints as are afforded in finitude. It is this aspect of God's satisfaction which becomes prehended by the new occasion, providing initial guidance toward its own becoming. Its power is that it is the only force in the occasion's beginning which has reference to everything else the occasion prehends. This reference gives it a dominance over the others in that it has a directive power needed by the occasion, and lacking anywhere else in the universe. It is in fact a creative power of God inaugurating the definiteness which is the fundamental prerequisite for actuality. This is God's providence for the world, which is identical with God's creativity in the world.

The eschatological reality in God is effective for the temporal overcoming of evil by offering to each becoming actuality an optimum mode for dealing with the influences it receives from its past. However, the structure of any satisfaction's transitional creativity allows us to be more specific with regard to general features which will qualify every aim of God given to the world.

In our discussion of satisfaction in relation to transitional creativity in Chapter VI, we pointed out that every satisfaction contains anticipatory feelings of its own repetition in the future, and that in higher grades of occasions, these feelings for repetition can be combined with an urge toward transformation in more inclusive patterns of harmony. The anticipatory feelings of God, the ultimately complex entity, combine repetitive and transformative aspects. We have already discussed the transformative elements of God's aims, inasmuch as each aim will reflect a novel way of harmonizing the energies of the immediate past actual world for any nascent occasion. The repetitive force of the aim is particularly important, since it qualifies the mode of transformation offered. As repetitive, each aim from God will carry the force of God's communal nature toward modes of community in the world. The full complexity of every aim of God, therefore, will always be toward more inclusive modes of community insofar as they are transformatively sustainable by the interrelated realities of the world from their varous standpoints.

The communal aspect of the aim of God offered to each becoming occasion follows from the communal nature of God's own satisfaction. God is everlastingly transforming a prehended world into that which it can be through divine power; this is an apotheosis of the world, as was discussed in our last chapter. Thus the satisfaction of God is essentially communal in a way far transcending that of every finite entity. When a finite entity achieves satisfaction, holding a diversity together in unity, that diversity is an objectified delimitation of the actual world. The subjectivity is relatively simple, relating to the occasion alone. But God, retaining the subjective immediacy of every prehended reality, is a complex subjectivity. God's subjectivity, unlike that of any other, incorporates the immediacies of many subjectivities, mediating to each the sense of the whole from its very inception within the divine nature. This complexity is required to achieve the reality of adventure, zest, beauty, truth, and peace. There is no aspect of God's satisfaction which is not communal, nor which does not bring the resources of the primordial vision to bear transformatively on that community. Thus the transitional effect of God's satisfaction, experienced by every standpoint in creation, must carry with it an echo of the divine reality in novel urges toward deeper and richer forms of well-being in finite community.

It belongs to God that the fullness of God's own satisfaction is of a form of community far transcending that which is possible within finitude alone. Yet the appetition for increasing complexity within God's unity is simultaneously God's providence for a world which will enter into that community in its own due time. God's desire for the world must be that in its own actuality it will already reflect God's nature to the highest degree possible, so that the world's apotheosis will require a minimum of transformation, being already in conformity with the divine nature. The transformation then would require merely the grounding of the actuality within the concrescent subjectivity of God, where it would experience unimaginable fulfillment of its future. Therefore, just as God's own satisfaction is of communal harmony, God's aims to the world inexorably must reflect the value of participating in and contributing to communal richness.

This is all to say that Whitehead's use of five qualities to describe the reality of God's being—adventure, zest, truth, beauty and peace —find their best summation in the word he uses to describe the power which achieves them, Eros, or love. The togetherness of all things in the infinite satisfaction of God is the ultimacy of love, pervading and transforming each participant through the power of God's own subjectivity. The aims for the world that spring from this divine love are themselves aims toward a richness of community, which is as much named by love in the finite world as in the divine reality.

This means, then, that every aim from God will be toward that which builds up the richness of community, and that the structure of temporal redemption will be and must be essentially communal. In a process world of interrelated existence, that which builds up the richness of community can in no sense be antithetical to the good of the individual, since the well-being of the individual enriches the community in which that individual participates: the one is for the many, and the many are for the one. The all-inclusive well-being of the many in community is the reflection of God's image in the world.

God's aim is given, continuously pushing toward the richness of communities of communities. Just here, however, one is reminded of Schleiermacher's portrayal of the problem of evil as the sense in which spiritual existence lags behind physical existence. If we translate his insight into process terms, we would say that the formation of community is like the process of concrescence writ large. We necessarily unite ourselves in groupings of societies within societies, each of which has its mode of satisfaction. Like entities, the society will project a force for its own perpetuation, but if it does not also project a force for transformation, then it parallels Schleiermacher's description of sheerly physical existence that does not go beyond its

self-concerns. The higher grades of satisfaction are increasingly transformative, so that they become a force not simply for perpetuation,
but for wider patterns of harmony beyond that which they can
achieve individually. If this becomes akin to Schleiermacher's description of spiritual existence, then one aspect of the problem of evil is
that in the evolution of societies, self-perpetuation must first be
established in order that there may be a basis for self-transcendence.
But self-transcendence toward a wider good may appear to conflict
with self-perpetuation, and societies refuse their own advancement.
The call of spiritual existence, of eschatological redemption on earth,
is that, like God, a society's transitional creativity will be adapted to
ever inclusive modes of well-being. That God calls us to such forms of
existence, with the call adapted to the particularities of each society
in its context, is built into the dynamics of the process metaphysics.
Whether or not we act creatively in history on the basis of these real
possibilities rests with our individual and corporate freedom to assent
to the initial aims of God.

This image of finite communities mirroring the nature of God is
admittedly visionary, approximated only in part by the various communities in the world. Yet it becomes fundamental to the structure of
temporal redemption since it speaks to possibilities for the world
emanating from the nature of God to work the world's good. It
bespeaks the providence of God for increasing opportunities for
intensities of harmony within the world. The redemptive reality of
God's communal nature is the ground of hope that the world, in all its
ambiguities of freedom and finitude, can nonetheless actualize itself
in congruity with God's aims. The communal structure of redemption is a constant given in the world, an unfailing resource for our
good.

There is yet one further aspect to the structure of temporal redemption that must be discussed before we turn more specifically to
an extension of the discussion of freedom begun in Chapter IV. This
has to do with the incompletion of being, already mentioned in
connection with Schleiermacher. Because of the ontological interrelationship of existence, no evil is simply private; every evil is a
public evil. Even to inflict harm upon the self is also to inflict harm
upon the larger society of relationships which are enriched or
impoverished by the well-being of each self; there is no private evil.
However, the corollary of this is that since all evil is social, no evil is
ever final; its effects continue. This entails that every present depends

upon the future for its completion, as was discussed in Chapter VI. Thus a basic element at work in the societal structure of redemption is the ability of the present to reinterpret the past. For example, one mode of social evil is legitimating the limitation of the good to but a few through a particular economic, political, and cultural system. Such a system depends upon each present for its perpetuation. Meaning depends upon context, and it rests within the power of the present to forge a new position which can, either singly or cumulatively, contribute a significantly altered dimension to the context such that the original value system is changed. The present continuously completes the past, but in the very completion of the past, the past can be transformed.[11]

A concrete illustration of this principle was given in Chapter IV through the account of the two women who sought ordination in the nineteenth century, but who were not accepted as ministers in their own time. Their contemporaries judged them as evil, as upsetting the established order of male and female roles. In the rejection, the established order was strengthened yet further. However, even though the society refused the women and what they represented, the society was indelibly affected by them. The women were as seeds of a revolution which would come to full growth long after they themselves had died. This revolution depended upon other voices taking up the cry, continuing to create that discordant note within society, and refusing to rest with the strengthened value which excluded women. One hundred years following society's rejection of the two women, they are heroines and pioneers of a movement calling far more successfully for the full inclusion of women within the social order. The inclusion, however, has ramifications far greater than simply admitting women into a previously restricted profession. The inclusion calls for adjustment in the economic, political, and personal orders of the society, bringing about the society's transformation toward a more inclusive mode of well-being. The infinality of evil, and the fluid nature of an ontologically interdependent society, is the structure that makes transformation possible in history.

Nietzsche called for a transvaluation of values; the relational structure of existence whereby the present has the power to transform the past is the context of transvaluation. Since the redemptive direction of the transvaluation is necessarily toward inclusiveness of well-being, a society open to transformation must engage in self-analysis from the perspective of those without well-being. What societal values perpetrate ill-being, and what societal systems ensure it? Transvaluation of values progresses toward inclusiveness of well-being, and a continuous restructuring of society toward that achievement. The incompleteness of all societies, whereby they must inexorably respond to discordancies within on the one hand, and to the complex aim of God toward deeper and richer community on the other, is the structure of societal redemption. Within the limitations and ambiguities of history, we are free to work creatively with that structure.

In Chapter IV we discussed the ambiguities of freedom in the context of finitude, relating freedom to the dynamics of the actual occasion. In this chapter, however, we have discussed the structure of temporal redemption primarily in communal terms: how is freedom exercised at that macracosmic level of the society, where social choices are made and suffered? How is it that with such a structure of redemption, orienting us toward richer modes of inclusive well-being, we nonetheless face the anomaly of socially created evil? Where is responsibility for such evil, and where is the realism in the hope for temporal redemption?

Every occasion is individual and social: it is itself, yet it comes into being by incorporating the energies of the many into its own concrescence. There is an inexorable interconnectedness within the world that is the basis for societal existence. Whitehead discusses in Part II of *Process and Reality* the organic connections creating societies of entities, whether rocks or persons, which have gradations of power for maximizing linkages that bring yet further social groupings into being. The defining characteristic of a society is the representation in each subset within it of common elements of form, ranging from the more general to the more specific; e.g., common citizenship in a nation, but divergent political affiliations, divergent geographical standpoints, divergent family and personal histories.

In our discussion of Schleiermacher above, we drew a parallel between the microcosmic dynamics of the occasion and the macrocosmic dynamics of the society.[12] The parallel must not be drawn too closely, since the society is a far looser organization than the concrescent entity. However, a comparison of the dynamics of the society of a person and the social groupings of communities and nations might offer fruitful analogies for considering societal freedom.

A person in a Whiteheadian framework is a complex society of societies, with groupings of occasions forming cells, organs, and bodily existence. In the complexity of personhood, there are various modes of coordination in the autonomic nervous system, and a dominant (but by no means all-powerful) coordinating agency in the series of occasions, highly open to novelty, constituting the seat of personality in the soul. The soul depends for its stability upon the groupings of occasions in the body, and the body depends upon the soul for novelty of purpose transcending the functions of any one part. Throughout the person there are varying degrees of freedom. Since no occasion is without freedom, and the person is constituted by many occasions, human freedom is not a simple thing, but a complex thing interdependently exercised within the living organism that is the person. Furthermore, not only is the freedom diffused through its shared quality, but it is also limited by inherited demands of conformity from the past, both in terms of personal and social history. In this system, the relative coordination of personal freedom and therefore the sense of identity falls to the soul. Since the soul is more open to novelty than any other aspect of the organism, the soul is the place of decision-making with regard to the degree of self-transcendence that will govern personal action. The connectedness with other persons and communities is fundamentally directed through freedom at this level.

If we attempt an analogy with civic society, constituted as it is by numerous subsocieties, the complexity and ambiguity of freedom increases dramatically. The more or less hidden complexity of freedom in personal existence comes far more dominantly to expression; freedom is more obviously shared, although the extent may be restricted. Just as in personal existence the many freedoms of occasions within the bodily organism are repressed within the autonomic system, even so in civic societies there may be a repression of vast masses of persons supporting the society. The perpetuation of the society, however, depends upon the continuation of the supportive environment. In personal existence, the supportive environment serves the total functioning of the person as directed through the soul; in civic existence, the analogous directing agency is the government. The freedom of the government can be expressed to the good of the whole or at the expense of the whole; it can direct itself solely to its internal well-being, ignoring its interdependent relations beyond itself, or it can incorporate into its purposes a transcendent element relating to the wider community of the world. Finally, this transcendent element may be toward engorgement of itself through absorption of

otherness, or it can be toward novel forms of communities of communities.

As to the question of responsibility for the use of societal freedom,
the personal analogy may again be helpful. God's aims come not
simply to the soul of a person, but to each occasion constituting that
person. Personal responsibility is correspondingly complex. Occasions with low tolerance for novelty respond more conformably to
God's aims, which in turn would be directed toward normal patterns
of growth within the limitations of context. Freedom is present, but
minimally. As the capacity for novelty increases, there are corre-
sponding increases in the variety of aims the occasion can receive, the
freedom of response in coordinating those aims relative to personal
existence, and responsibility with respect to self and others for the
decisions thus made. To extend the analogy to civic existence, every
agent within the society receives aims from God relative to self and
context, with a communal force inherent in every aim. To that
extent, every agent within the society is resposible for the work of
the society, but not to the same degree. Those who act in leadership
positions within the society, in whatever political form the society
may take, are functionally analogous to the soul in personal existence, and bear the greater responsibility for responding to God's continuously given aims toward forms of inclusive well-being in communal existence. But in no case does the greater responsibility of the
leadership abrogate the responsibility of the society as a whole, any
more than the dominance of the soul can allow dismissal of the freedoms within the supporting body.

To continue the analogy, drawing on the discussion of evil in
Chapter IV, neither civic society nor the person acts in a sheerly
contemporaneous context: both bear the weight of inheritance,
limiting the possibilities for what might be in the evolution of the
world toward richer modes of communal existence. Inheritance has
its greatest force in its demand for conformal feelings of repetition.
For person or civic society, strength of repetition establishes the
accepted and often unquestioned norms governing the sensibilities of
the day. Insofar as these are repeated, responsibility for that repetition
belongs to the personal and societal present, for good or for ill, depending upon the relation of the norms to inclusiveness of well-being.

The redemptive aims of God toward societies, therefore, must be of
great complexity, directed throughout the society and accounting for
great varieties of purpose. But there will be an inevitable aspect to

every aim relating to inclusiveness of well-being in the society and the world as a whole. Social responsibility belongs to the whole society, with varied degrees of freedom to exercise that responsibility.

The freedom to work within the temporal structure of redemption thus rests with participants in the societies of the world. No utopia may be reached: the limitations of freedom and finitude discussed in Chapter IV preclude it. But if these limitations are taken as authorization for complacency with regard to societal evil, we fall from the image of God and increase our everlasting and historical responsibility for evil. Every form of the good is limited and calls for its own transcendence, and the recognition of ill-being in society is itself a call to transform our notions and realizations of the good toward increasing circles of well-being. The power of God so guides us, and the structure of temporal redemption assists us. As in a Kantian model, the possibility to do good is the responsibility to do good.

The implications for Christian theology of this metaphysical description move toward a primacy of ecclesiology, such that the incarnation of God in the world is precisely the revelation of God as love within human community.[13] This revelation is for the sake of empowering the creation of specific communities within the larger society that will manifest and foster deeper and deeper intensities of love. These communities, like God, are to manifest an actualized love among their members. But just as the love which is in God cannot be contained, so must the love in these communities go beyond their own borders. The well-being which is within must pour forth as a directed influence toward the well-being of all, serving the wider society. The boundaries of these communities, like the boundaries of God, are to be open, pouring forth an energy for good beyond themselves. The center of love which forms the core of the communities must influence the creation of goodness among all communities.[14] The specific nature of the goodness to be created is not the specific province of any one community, but is to be transformatively created by all. Every form of goodness is open to its own transcendence.

That there should be many communities follows from the image of God which is envisioned. God is a complex subjectivity, containing many subjectivities within the depths of the one divine immediacy. God is intensive; the reflection of God in the world must be extensive. The many-within-one must issue into a oneness-among-many. First, the communities of God will contain an intimacy within each community as a whole, where many are together as one. Each community will be marked by the uniqueness of its finite context, embodying a very particular vision of how to be community in the world. Second, the communities together must interrelate in such a way that the separate integrity of each community is valued, enriching the community of communities. Third, the network of communities shall ever be open to systems which either define themselves outside of community, or are so different as to form no definite communal bond perceivable to the communities. In this threefold concern, core communities in the world variously manifest complementing unities of adventure, zest, truth, beauty, and peace in a moving image of divine love, to the good of all.

Within a process world, to speak about temporal redemption as increasingly inclusive communities of well-being requires that we make explicit, rather than implicit, the breadth of this inclusiveness. In an interrelated world, where societies are more than simply human groups but include the enormous complexity of the earth as a whole—and the universe beyond it—inclusiveness of well-being refers to all existence, human and nonhuman, living and nonliving. While there may be a gradation of value based on increased complexity of existence, there is no existent society or entity devoid of value. The redemptive community must look to the care of the earth in its vision of inclusive well-being.

There is a redemptive work to be done. Social evils rise in the ambiguity of the good which can be accomplished for some through the oppression of others, or, as Walter Rauschenbusch so succinctly put it, the problem with evil is that it is profitable.[15] Societal evil is the responsibility of the whole society, but the specifically redemptive communities within the larger society have a unique role in holding forth the norm of a dynamic inclusiveness of well-being in community. As such, they are called to be catalysts of transformation in the world, pointing to the evils of limiting mutual well-being to but a chosen segment of the society.

Insofar as a redemptive community itself models the openness of God's peace, it becomes a concrete lure for the good. It is itself a change in the environment which affects all other finite reality, becoming a force which must be accounted for throughout the larger society. Further, insofar as God is faithful in providing all societies with aims which are as consonant as possible with the divine nature, the redemptive society labors with God, increasing the possibilities for redemption in the world. The redemptive society not only models God's peace within its own community, but it also creates an openness for changes in other societies through the dual participation of its members in several societies. There is an essential openness to the redemptive community. This openness is actualized as its members receive strength from one another, and go forth to their work in the surrounding societies, bringing their vision to bear upon their work.

Confrontation is also the task of the redemptive community, both by its individual members and corporately. The community has the opportunity to be that discordant note within the larger society that utilizes the essentially fluid nature of the society to bring about transformation. The corporate influence of the redemptive community/communities as a whole is particularly important, since the rootedness of social evil in the mores of a culture defies single efforts toward transformation. Social organizations are needed to redress social evil.

The redemptive community is called to actualize a moving image of God within its own structures, with a mutality of good and inclusiveness of well-being. The faithfulness of God ensures that guidance is ever given toward the form of this structure, and also that the actual form will be dynamic rather than static, moving always to fuller modes of community. Since God is a self-surpassing manifestation of increasingly complex modes of harmony, no finite mode can possibly be called final. Its situation in finitude, as discussed in Chapter IV, precludes its own ultimacy, and the very model of God precludes its finality. Thus each redemptive community is called to open itself to the novelty of transformation, and to be an agent for the transformation of social ills. The horrors of our time, whether holocaust or nuclear threat or political oppression or social oppression, are themselves a call to the redemptive community to cast its corporate influence toward the well-being of the whole world, seeking always the increase of well-being in varieties of communities.

Thus the structure of redemption speaks to the possibilities for the good in the human situation, with all its ambiguities of freedom and finitude. This structure speaks to the evil following from finitude which Schleiermacher named as the incompletion of being. For Schleiermacher, as for Whitehead, the world is marked by interdependence moving toward a conscious recognition of that interdependence, and action in accordance with interdependence. For Whitehead as well as for Schleiermacher, the world evolves slowly, stumbling toward its destiny, but incapable of achieving it alone. The reality of interdependence is the world's vulnerability and the world's richness, its possibility of beauty and its belatedness in achieving that beauty. Insofar as the world does not live out of conscious celebration of its interdependence, it is mired in the problem of evil.

For Schleiermacher, redemptive completion came through the incarnation of Jesus Christ, fulfilling in his own person that which was the destiny of the race. The reality of that fulfillment drew all the interrelated world into its accomplishment, and catalytically established the community called to continue that fulfillment in history. For Whitehead, completion also comes through incarnation, but metaphysically this is expressed through the incarnation of God's providence for every creature through the initial aim. The incarnation of God in the world is followed by the incarnation of the world in God. Rather than precluding a specific incarnation, this lays a groundwork for it and for the power that its intensity of revelation can unleash for redemptive communities in the world. The completion which comes about has a dynamic, everlasting quality in God. In the world, completion is qualified by the freedom of the future. It calls for a trust beyond the self toward communal good. Incompletion in the structure of redemption is a transition through trust to a wholeness that transcends the boundaries of personality.

Alienation as evil also receives the hope of its overcoming in history through the mediation of community. There is a deep sense in which alienation is written into the structure of things, since the rhythm of the universe moves from the many to the one to the many again. The one, inexorably alone in its concrescent freedom, is caught between the relations of past and future. There is no direct relation with contemporaries, given the relativity of time and process, so that metaphysically the entity is alone in the privacy of its becoming. The grounds for existential loneliness and alienation are real indeed.

And yet in a process universe this alienation is a moment, the breathing space of the universe, as it moves from relation to unification to relation again. The solitariness of the one is yet filled with the intimacy of the communal relations which enter into its becoming, making its becoming possible. And the fruit of its solitariness is its own gift to the community again. The transitoriness of finite being is itself an answer to metaphysical alienation: existence is a movement from relation to relation, so that the solitariness is indeed but one aspect of the movement. Openness to the community in trust increases the receptivity to the influences of the many, and optimizes the zest of becoming in anticipation of its communal effects.

In a transitory world, Nietzsche could note the threat of meaning-lessness and aimlessness haunting even the most vibrant affirmation of values doomed to perish. The everlasting structure of redemption in God is the primary answer to such evils, but temporal redemption is also given. And again, the community is the redemptive structure. Meaning in the creative affirmation of the past, aims given through the creative formation of a future which is destined for God, and a togetherness which is not arbitrary, but which is integral to the very structure of the most individual being—all these become the work of a community in relation to an individual, and the individual in relation to a community. In such a setting these evils can be answered with hope and creativity. Action in accordance with such hope infuses the finite world with a meaning within itself, from itself, and beyond itself. The structure within which these possibilities are brought to fruition is the structure of the many individuals recognizing their interdependence in community.

Freedom in community, the many toward the one toward the many again, provides the finite context wherein obstruction and destruction can occur, and yet it provides as well the finite context where healing and redemption are brought to bear. The social nature of every entity, and the necessary reliance on an indeterminate future for the completion of meaning, become necessary consider-ations in the understanding of evil. But these realities are just as necessary for the understanding of temporal redemption. The achievement of temporal redemption depends upon both the conditions of the world which support it to a greater or lesser degree, and upon the freedom within each concrescent reality of the world to actualize the mode of redemptive harmony God has offered. Insofar as the world acts responsibly and responsively, its actuality is a rich gift to God and to history.

Given our dependence on social forms of existence, it is no wonder that visions of redemption have been formulated throughout Chris-tian history with the image of a City, whether Augustine's City of God or Kant's ethical commonwealth of hearts. In this process vision, too, the notion of a city dominates, expressed now through the language of community. God *is* that city, that community, of a redeemed and transformed earth, making possible for us temporal cities reflecting that great inclusiveness of well-being. God's own freedom ensures that the everlasting city is actual, manifesting in infinite patterns of self-surpassing beauty the reconciliation of all things in God. Finite freedom, exercised within the ambiguities of history and in cooperation with God's unfailing aim, make dim reflections of that divine city possible in our own histories. There is ground to the hope for an enriched and enriching world community, as "what is done in the world is transformed into a reality in heaven, and the reality of heaven passes back into the world."

VIII

The Metaphysics of the Redemptive God

hroughout our discussion of eschatology, whether everlasting or historical, I have indicated much concerning a doctrine of God. This vision is of a God infinitely complex, incorporating the world into the divine self in an apotheosis which is the judgment and redemption of the world. This action within God has a redemptive effect upon the world, making possible for that world a new reflection of the divine image.

Throughout, the categories of Whitehead's process philosophy have been utilized to give expression to the vision. The ability of this philosophy to tend equally to the two poles of the interpretation of evil—finitude and freedom—make this philosophy uniquely suitable for the purposes of envisioning how evil may be answered. Central to the vision, of course, is the doctrine of God. This final chapter incorporates the aspects of God which have been developed in the previous chapters, and probes the metaphysical structures which support such an understanding of God.

Whitehead's model for understanding the dynamics of any reality is that of the actual entity. This is a dynamic process of becoming in which the data of the past are unified through contrast, comparison, and delimitation until they yield the single reality that is the new entity. The response to the past is termed the physical pole, and the dynamic of unification springs from the mental pole. The mental pole is the feeling for that which the entity might become; it functions as an immediate future which, in conjunction with the past, creates the present. The process by which the mental pole governs the unification of data is concrescence, and the directive element is called the entity's subjective aim for its own becoming. The result of this process is the attainment of the goal, termed satisfaction. This satisfaction is also a call for a future beyond the entity itself that will perpetuate the entity's value. Entity succeeds entity, or as Whitehead put it, "the many become one, and are increased by one."[1]

In the previous chapters we have discussed this process in some detail relative to creativity, arguing for concrescent creativity, the creativity of enjoyment, and transitional creativity. The subjectivity of the entity is located in the first two modes of creativity, and its objectivity is created relative to its finite future through transitional creativity. It belongs to the process that only when satisfaction is attained—and the entity becomes the definiteness of a fully resolved concrescence —is the entity available to others through transitional creativity.

This model of the actual entity, describing the dynamics of existence, is also the model for developing metaphysically the structure of divine existence. However, throughout *Process and Reality*, Whitehead calls attention to the difference which obtains between God as an actual entity and the finite entities. Whereas the finite entities, called "occasions" by Whitehead, originate from the physical pole (the feeling of other entities), God originates from the mental pole.[2] In God, this pole is called the primordial nature, and is portrayed as an eternal envisagement or valuation of all possibilities. These possibilities are devoid of subjectivity, and hence Whitehead terms them "eternal objects." They are potentialities for existence, the infinitely varied possibilities and combinations of possibilities which could conceivably qualify any actuality.

This difference in origination between God and occasions is not arbitrary, nor does it violate Whitehead's metaphysical principles. On the contrary, the metaphysical scheme requires such a differentiation even while it demands that the differentiation take place within the general requirements of existence briefly described above. The continual thrust of the world toward novelty cannot find its explanation solely in the completed occasions making up the beginning occasion's past actual world. Since novelty significantly occurs, and since Whitehead's system requires that the reasons for things rest within actuality, the novelty of the world demands a grounding in some actuality.

However, the occasion itself does not provide sufficient ground to account for novelty on either the microcosmic or the macrocosmic level. Its own concrescence is derived finitely from prehensions of other occasions in its past world. Its conceptualizations must have reference to this world, but its degree of novelty may far surpass this essential givenness. What is the reasonable ground of such novelty? Furthermore, on the macrocosmic level the advance of nature is coordinated in its reach toward new types of existence in a way that goes beyond the ability of any single occasion to explain. Hence the macrocosmic process toward novelty is likewise inexplicable on the level of the occasion alone.

What is needed is an activating link between potentiality as a whole and the process of the world, whether in reference to the coordinated advance of nature, or the single process of the finite occasion's coming into being. The link, however, must be actual, real, and, therefore, related to the dynamics which describe actuality. Otherwise, the "deus ex machina" nature of the explanation renders it arbitrary and incoherent. Thus the activating principle of novelty must be an actual entity.

Given these requirements, the notion of an actual entity originating from an eternal conceptualization and valuation of all possibility is necessary for the coherence of the system. It completes the description of the universe in consonance with the general understanding, not in violation or transcendence of it. This consonance is demonstrated in that the understanding of God in terms of an actual entity complies with the general structures for all entities, even though exhibiting these in a different order. This different order is that stated: "the origination of God is from the mental pole, the origination of an actual occasion is from the physical pole" (PR 36).

It is fundamentally important to consider the consequences of God's origination in the mental pole. Whitehead indicates these consequences at the close of *Process and Reality* by stating, "In every respect God and the world move conversely to each other in respect to their process" (PR 349). The difference in origination naturally requires a difference in the process of concrescence itself, and this difference is sufficient to account for God's ability to incorporate other occasions in their immediacy within the divine concrescence, to influence the world during concrescence, and to be understood as the everlasting and ever living entity.

A clear investigation of the occasion's process of concrescence will allow us to move toward the implications of reversal. The becoming of an occasion is the integration of many prehensions into one final, determinate feeling, with this feeling being the satisfaction and completion of the occasion. Among Whitehead's approaches to describing this process is that in which he analyzes it in terms of four phases: datum, process, satisfaction, and decision.[3] The terminal poles in this description, datum and decision, look respectively toward the past and toward the future; they indicate the inescapably relational nature of the process. They are related to being rather than to becoming, since "datum" relates to the accomplished being of the once-becoming past, and "decision" relates to the manner in which the concrescing occasion will become a being, a stubborn fact, or the future. The intervening states, concrescence and satisfaction, describe the novel synthesis of the past into a dynamic present. Beginning from the decisions of the past, the occasion moves toward its own decision for the future. The movement itself, the subjectivity, must be understood through these two middle terms, process and satisfaction.

Whitehead dwells at some length on the peculiarity of an entity's satisfaction: it is in a sense both a part of the process, and outside of the process. On the one hand, the satisfaction is the whole modus operandi of the entity—the aim toward just that satisfaction is the principle of concrescence, and one cannot therefore entirely divorce the satisfaction from the process. It has been the determing factor of the process, the "lure" of the occasion's becoming. But on the other hand,

[satisfaction] cannot be construed as a component contributing to its own concrescence.... It is the outcome separated from the process, thereby losing the actuality of the atomic entity, which is both process and outcome.... But the 'satisfaction' is the 'superject' rather than the 'substance' or the 'subject.' It closes up the entity: and yet is the superject adding its character to the creativity whereby there is a becoming of entities superseding the one in question. The 'formal' reality of the actuality in question belongs to its process of concrescence and not to its 'satisfaction.' This is the sense in which the philosophy of organism interprets Plato's phrase 'and never really is'; for the superject can only be interpreted in terms of its objective immortality (PR 84).

Thus while an entity must be considered in terms of its satisfaction, its satisfaction nevertheless transcends it. The satisfaction marks the internal completion of the entity, and begins the process of transition whereby the occasion becomes effective for others. The concrescence of the occasion, then, is creativity governed by the desire toward satisfaction; it is the growth toward a determinate value. During the process, the nature of the satisfaction becomes increasingly clear to the subject through the modifications it effects.

In the primary phase of the subjective process, there [is] a conceptual feeling of subjective aim: the physical and other feelings originate as steps towards realizing this conceptual aim through their treatment of initial data. This basic conceptual feeling suffers simplification in the successive phases of the concrescence. It starts with conditioned alternatives, and by successive decisions is reduced to coherence (PR 224).

This simplification which takes place by no means refutes the complexity of the final satisfaction. The occasion remains an intricate fact which must be explained as much through the many prehensions which conditioned the satisfaction as through the internal process whereby these prehensions were unified. Throughout the many comparisons and integrations of feelings, the occasion can be understood as moving from many to one, from a dimly held preference amidst many possibilities toward a decisive affirmation of the unified value it has become. Reduction and simplification toward an increasing determinateness mark the process of concrescence. Thus from the many datum of the past, a process of integration comes into being which yields a satisfaction; this satisfaction is both goal and guidance of the process. With the process completed, the satisfaction provides a concrete decision which is evocative, demanding that it be data for a next moment of becoming.

But God does not originate from data received from a past—were that so, God would also need an explanation for novelty, and we would be in an infinite regress. Rather, God "originates" in a decision which is a primordial valuation of all possibilities; Whitehead calls this an envisagement which contains within it an appetition for realization in actuality. Thus the satisfaction of God lies in this conceptual atemporality; it is primordial, underlying and pervading the reality of God. This being the case, the concrescence of God cannot move *toward* satisfaction; it can only move *from* satisfaction. Nor can it move toward an increasing simplification of data and subjective aim; it must move instead toward an ever increasing complexity in continual and dynamic realization of that satisfaction. This requires a constantly expanding complexity to God rather than a simplification. The superjective appetition of satisfaction becomes the means whereby such complexity is achieved. While such a statement might at first appear to be a violation of Whitehead's principles, I hope to show that given the beginnings of God in the conceptual nature, the converse is so: the principles would be violated if the reversal of concrescence did not hold.

To explicate this further, we must consider the manner in which the conceptual origination coincides with the satisfaction of God. This can be done by elaborating on some of Whitehead's direct statements to this effect.

By the principle of relativity, there can only be one non-derivative actuality, unbounded by its prehensions of an actual world. Such a primordial superject of creativity achieves, in its unity of satisfaction, the complete conceptual valuation of all eternal objects (*PR* 32).

And again:

The 'superjective' nature of God is the character of the pragmatic value of his specific satisfaction qualifying the transcendent creativity in the various temporal instances (*PR* 88).

Clearly, God's primordial nature is here directly related to both satisfaction and superjectivity. Since God's origination is just here in the primordial nature, God also originates, conversely to the occasion, in both satisfaction and superjectivity. What is the end with the occasion is the beginning with God.[4]

The satisfaction of God's conceptualization results from the completeness of this conceptualization. There is no potentiality that is not felt eternally by God. Since each potentiality, in its very mode of possibility, is related to every other potentiality either through pattern or diversity, the completeness of God's feeling allows an absolute valuation of each potentiality in all mode of relatedness. Since all that could be, in any conceivable manner or mode, is thus included, the valuation simply must be at the same time a satisfaction.

Whitehead speaks at times of this valuation as if it is not actual, and for that reason one might infer that it is not strictly a satisfaction. The envisagement is called "deficient in actuality" (*PR* 34), and the concrescence of God might then be considered more analogous to an occasion's drive toward an actual, determinate value. But this cannot be the whole story, for the very reason that the eternal envisagement of the eternal objects takes place within God, who is most certainly an actual entity. By virtue of God's actuality, the satisfaction which is the valuation of the objects must be an actual satisfaction, regardless of the fact that it is necessary for this satisfaction to manifest itself in increasing complexity. There is no actual deficiency in God's valuation—only in the abstraction of considering God in the partiality of the conceptual nature alone could the satisfaction be considered less than actual.

By accepting the initial satisfaction of God, we must then develop its implications for concrescence. Otehwise, we are left with an absurdity: the final satisfaction would have to be either the same as that which was determinately valued in God's primordial beginnings, in which case the concrescence is superfluous, or else the difference in the satisfaction would entail the contradiction of being an impossible satisfaction, lying beyond all primordial possibilities. The completeness of the primordial vision and the valuation attendant on this completeness prohibits any understanding of God's concrescence as a series of reductions whereby a novel determinate feeling is achieved.

In further confirmation of this, note how Whitehead's description of the phases within an occasion's becoming compare with his description of God's primordial nature.

There are three successive phases of feelings, namely, a phase of conformal feelings, one of 'conceptual' feelings, and one of 'comparative' feelings, including 'propositional' feelings in this last species....

The two latter stages of feeling are the stages of comparison; these stages involve comparisons, and comparisons of comparisons; and the admission, or exclusion, of an indefinite complexity of potentialities for comparison, in ascending grades.

The ultimate attainment is 'satisfaction' (PR 164, 166).

Here the process of concrescence is stated in such a way that the two latter stages lead to what appears to be a final valuation of the eternal objects relevant to the occasion. But if the final satisfaction is indeed the result of the progressive gradation of eternal objects relative to the occasion throughout its concrescence, then the satisfaction is quite analogous to the primordial gradation in God. Again, the end of the occasion is the "beginning" of God. The primordial satisfaction directs rather than concludes God's concrescence.

At this point we need to consider Whitehead's already quoted statement to the effect that a satisfaction cannot be a component in the process of an occasion, and ask if the objection still holds with God. There are two points at issue. First, a satisfaction that was a component in the process would never truly be complete, for it would require successive modifications according to the new data made available through its relative effectiveness. But second, and underlying our first issue, is the violence done to the givenness of the past, and hence the whole analysis of process and relativity. The inclusion of the satisfaction in the occasion's process as a contributory component would amount to a return to a metaphysics not of process, but of a single substance which undergoes accidental changes. The insight into the dynamism of existence wherein relations are internal to every actuality would be lost.

However, such a consequence is avoided because of the very completeness of God's primordial satisfaction. The difficulty of the changing nature of the satisfaction which would occur if it were a component of concrescence is owing to the limited initial selectivity of the finite occasion. In its finitude, the occasion must negatively prehend many eternal objects in order to achieve its final complex unity. But if the occasion experienced the effects of its satisfaction, then previously irrelevant objects would move into relevance, and a necessary alteration would take place. This is the point where the givenness of the occasion as past would be overthrown.

But Whitehead quite explicitly states that God's primordial nature is "infinite, devoid of all negative prehensions" (*PR* 345). Since God's conceptual valuation involves positively every conceivable possibility, eliminating none through negative prehensions, there is no way in which the satisfaction of the envisagement can be essentially altered. In this case, the satisfaction of God can be a component of the divine nature without requiring any deviation from the satisfaction or consequent change in God's essential character. There simply are no new possibilities which could alter the satisfaction. Therefore, only when a satisfaction is concerned with the partial envisagement of a finite occasion would the fundamental principles of process break down; in the completeness of God's vision, such a breakdown cannot occur.

Further, as we discussed in Chapter VI, the satisfaction of God is qualitative in nature. It is the primacy of a harmony in which each part contributes to and benefits from the ordering of the whole, with all the resources of the primordial ordering brought to bear in the achievement of that harmony. Thus the satisfaction of God is complete, since it is the fullness of all possibility and all actuality in transformative union, and yet demands further completion, manifesting itself in an everlasting transformation of reality after reality. It is a satisfaction which is in principle dynamic and unending; an enjoyment ever generating a moving intensity of its own actualization.

How, then, does this primordial satisfaction affect God's concrescence, and what is its bearing on the eschatology we have described?

The answer lies in the superjectivity which accompanies God's satisfaction, and in the converse movement from simplicity to an expanding complexity and concreteness. Such expanding complexity in no
way undercuts the unity of God, since the complexity is governed by
God's satisfaction and hence subjective aim. For just as the subjective
aim of the finite occasion is inexorably related to its ultimate satisfaction, even so with God. For the occasion, the subjective aim issues
into satisfaction, and yet has been evoked at its very beginning by the
possibility of that satisfaction. For God, the subjective aim issues *from*
satisfaction, ensuring that the prehended world will enter into a
manifestation of that satisfaction. The unity of the subjective aim
unites the complex prehensions of God into the harmony of the
primordial satisfaction. "God is primordially one, namely, the primordial unity of relevance of the many potential forms: in the process,
God acquire a consequent multiplicity, which the primordial character absorbs into its own unity" (PR 349).

Because of the primordial satisfaction, God always prehends the
world in the full consciousness of purposive valuation.[5] This is, of
course, the converse of the occasion, which initially prehends its world
in a state of relative indeterminateness, using these prehensive feelings
in the modification of its aim. It is impossible for God's prehensions to
modify the divine aim, since it is eternally primordial; therefore, God
prehends the world not for the determination of the aim but for the
manifestation of the aim. The occasions of the world are prehended
for what they can be, given the aim. God feels each occasion in terms
of how it can fulfill the primordial will toward harmony.

The primordial aim is therefore directive of the concrescence of
God in determining how an occasion will be or can be modified to fit
the aim, rather than being itself modified through the occasions. But
note that, as was discussed in the previous chapter, the aim is
qualitative and not specific in the details as to how this quality will be
further concretized. The occasions contribute their own uniqueness
of exclusive value to the harmony of God's nature. It is *this* occasion,
in all its specificity, which is prehended in such a way that it
participates in the aim of God. The harmony of God is a harmony
involving the particularity which has been achieved through the
multiple creativity of the finite world. Since occasions are constantly
being multiplied, the harmony is dynamic; there can be no static
pattern of divine harmony, since the pattern changes with every
prehension. What remains as constant is that the occasion is

prehended into a harmony which everlastingly manifests the determinate value of God's primordial nature.

While God's satisfaction issues in the subjective aim of continually concretizing that satisfaction through God's prehensions, this satisfaction is also simultaneously superjective. God, as that entity originating in the complete conceptual envisagement, is also continually "consequent." As an actual entity, God is always conceptual, always physical; always superjective, always prehensive: the sequence is logical and analytical rather than actual in the sense that God would not be an actual entity—and therefore would not be anything—if not primordial and consequent simultaneously. A primordial nature cannot exist alone.

The essential unity of God is understood by Whitehead in that section of *Process and Reality* where he epitomizes the "primordial," the "consequent," and the "superjective" natures, for no nature is described without reference to one of the other two.[6] The primordial nature is described in the context of a concrescence that relates to the consequent nature (the feeling for basic conditions in the world) and the superjective nature (the lure relevant to the future of the world). The consequent nature is a physical prehension of the actualities in the universe that is directed by the primordial nature and, we are told elsewhere, leads to a unification of these actualities with the primordial nature. The superjective nature is the pragmatic effectiveness of the primordial satisfaction as it is manifested through the consequent nature. Primordial, consequent, and superjective aspects of God thus each require reference to the others for the fullest explication of each. God is a unity, but the complex unity of an actual entity, and hence the fullest understanding of the "natures" is simply an understanding of the divine nature. God is not consecutively primordial, consequent, and superjective, but simultaneously primordial, consequent, and superjective. The primordial has a logical priority, since it is foundational in that God does not originate from a world of physical actualities. But God as the primordial creature is necessarily concrescent and superjective.

We must give further attention to this superjectivity entailed by the primordial satisfaction. Despite the peculiarities involved in a concrescence which is the converse of an occasion's, the same metaphysical realities are exemplified in both God and the occasions. The superjectivity of God must therefore be similar to finite superjectivity. in the temporal occasion, superjectivity (or transitional creativity) is derived from the occasion's own feeling for the future; in the following passages Whitehead seems to indicate that the same principle holds for God:

For the perfected actuality [the ultimate unity of the multiplicity of actual fact with the primordial conceptual fact] passes back into the temporal world, and qualifies this world so that each temporal actuality includes it as an immediate fact of relevant experience (PR 351).

The 'superjective' nature of God is the character of the pragmatic value of his specific satisfaction qualifying the transcendent creativity in the various temporal instances (PR 88).

The occasion's satisfaction "adds its character to the creativity whereby there is a becoming of entities superseding the one in question" (PR 84); its determination of value requires a new unification in the world. God's satisfaction is primordially one, achieving a continuously expanding complexity as God absorbs the world into multiple unifications within the divine nature. The quality of God's satisfaction does not change since it is always harmony, always adventure, zest, and peace. But the components of this satisfaction are continuously increasing, and each addition to the pattern qualifies the superjectivity of the satisfaction relative to the becoming world. Since each addition is received by God in conformation with the overarching subjective aim, the quality of God's satisfaction never changes; it is impossible that any of the qualities mentioned above should be lacking. But the concrete actuality of just how these qualities are manifested has changed and is always changing. This is the source of the manifold specificity of God's superjective nature, the "how" by which God feels novel possibilities pertaining to the immediate future of the temporal world. This is the sense in which God's satisfaction issues into superjectivity which is always relevant to the world.

God's prehensions of the world conform the occasions to the divine satisfaction, for God feels the occasions for what they can be within that harmony, and manifests this harmony through precisely these occasions. Just as the finite occasion prehends its past actual world comparatively, valuing each prehension with a "mutuality of subjective form" which is the feeling of each in relation to all others, so does God. And just as the finite occasion contrasts these feelings with a subjective aim toward its own becoming, so does God. The difference in God is that the mutuality of subjective form is *already* in terms of a subjective aim of harmony which is manifested in that subjective form. Thus each prehended occasion is felt in relation to all others in ordered forms of harmony, as was discussed in Chapter VI. This beginning of its participation in the concrescence of God is a concretization of God's satisfaction which is of immediate relevance to the becoming world, as was discussed in Chapter VII. God's enjoyment of this satisfaction includes a feeling for the successiveness made possible in the ongoing finite world as a result of this satisfaction. In other words, God's appetition is as complex as God's satisfaction. It is both an appetition toward its own continuing manifestation within the divine reality, and an appetition toward its effects on the world, which will itself, in its own turn, enter into that divine reality. The appetition toward the world stems from the mode of satisfaction relative to the immediate inclusion of the world in God. Since this is a continuous inclusion of all completed realities, the dynamic appetition toward the world is always multiple, impinging on every possible standpoint in the becoming world. The edges of God yield the future of the becoming world; the center of God yields the future of God.

The continuing concrescence of God, as was discussed in Chapter VI, moves the prehended world into ever deeper modes of manifesting the primodial vision. For the finite occasion, the movement of concrescence is from complexity to simplicity; the opposite is so for God. The simplest aspect of the divine concrescence is the initial prehension of the world in every "moment" of the divine life. The comparisons of each prehension with all other newly prehended occasions is the "first" phase of manifesting the divine harmony, and the phase which is immediately relevent to the world. It is a comparison which is harmonized through the resources of the primordial vision. Subsequent phases in this genetic analysis, however, take the comparison deeper into the wholeness of God, relating each occasion not only to its "might have been" from the primordial nature, but also to the adventure of the whole past world's destiny in God. The concrescence of God is the transformation of the world within the depths of God until the world participates fully in the manifestation of the primordial vision. But of course this is a dynamic harmony, in principle incapable of exhaustion, since the primordial vision is infinitely manifestable, and infinitely increasing in its complexity through the continuous addition of ever new occasions from the world.

Whereas the finite occasion achieves definiteness only at the conclusion of concrescence, and hence is only a superject for prehension by others upon completion of its concrescent process, the opposite is so with God. God "begins" with a definiteness which is constantly moving. The pattern of definiteness by its very nature is kaleidoscopic, manifesting one bright beauty following another, in ever self-surpassing intensity. The constancy is that the pattern always manifests the harmony of adventure, zest, peace, truth, and beauty; but *what* is manifesting these qualities, and *how*, is consequent upon God's prehension of the world. The definiteness, however, depends upon the primordial satisfaction and is mediated through the mutuality of subjective form by which God feels every prehended occasion in light of all others and in light of the primordial vision. Thus the initial harmony of the prehended occasions participates in the definiteness of God's satisfaction, and yields a twofold appetition for a future: an appetition for its repetition in the world, which constitutes God's providence through the initial aims, and an appetition for the deepening intensity of the divine nature through just these prehended occasions. God's satisfaction is a dynamic enjoyment of ever deepening intensity, always complete, and always in the process of completion.

Thus God anticipates the occasions of the world through the appetition which is the superjective nature, following from God's satisfaction. God does not prehend an anticipated occasion until it has reached its own creative satisfaction. But the conditions whereby the occasion may prehend God follow from the reversed concrescence of God. God's satisfaction is primordial and definite, whereas the occasions of the world manifest a satisfaction which is final and definite. Since determinateness and objectifiability are required for prehension, there is no categoreal reason why God may not be prehended by an occasion, despite the fact that the divine concrescence is everlasting, and hence "with" all occasions. God's conceptual beginning and satisfaction make all the difference in this regard.

A possible objection could be raised in that both God and the nascent occasion prehend the past upon its completion. Is there a problem in time here? Is not God's prehension of the just completed past contemporaneous with the new occasion's prehension of that past? If so, how does God's incorporation of that prehension into the divine satisfaction have relevance to the new occasion—isn't God too late for an initial aim? In Chapter V we spoke of the occasion's creative enjoyment of satisfaction as a shimmering in time, a breathing space between concrescent creativity and transitional creativity. There is a sense in which God surrounds the occasion but does not pervade the occasion. God anticipates the occasion through the initial aim, and awaits the outcome of that occasion's own decision. Having anticipated the occasion, God also waits in readiness for the outcome. God, unlike the finite, does not have to be evoked by the occasion's completion. Thus in that moment of definiteness which is the enjoyed determinacy of the occasion, God's "withness" is the sharing of that full enjoyment through subjective prehension. As the occasion generates transitional creativity, it is matched with the transitional creativity of God, and both together evoke the future.

Through the introduction of the sense of pastness which obtains between God and concrescing occasions, some dicussion of God's relation to time and space is required. We are presenting God as having an appetition toward an immediate future. However, God is nontemporal; how does God feel a future—or the spatiality which is integrally related to temporality?

The primary sense in which God can be neither temporal nor spatial lies in the everlastingly concrescent nature. Both time and space are connected by Whitehead to the passage of occasions—both become measures of the transitional creativity of the occasions. Time is "perpetual perishing," marking the completion of one entity and the beginning of another. Space is the atomization of the potential extensive continuum, and is likewise dependent upon the completion of entities.

The actual entities atomize it [the extensive continuum] and thereby make real what was antecedently merely potential. The atomization of the extensive continuum is also its temporalization; that is to say, it is the process of the becoming of actuality into what in itself is merely potential (PR 72).

Time and space in the sense in which we generally know them are therefore abstractions from the givenness of completed occasions. God, as everlastingly concrescent, never attains the staticity required to become a component part of spatio/temporal measurement; God is in this sense neither temporal nor spatial.

But there are two other senses of temporality to be considered. God is never static in givenness, since the divine satisfaction is dynamic. God therefore enjoys the second type of fluency which Whitehead contrasts with transitional creativity and perpetual perishing, the fluency of internal concrescence. The everlastingness of God, and the successiveness which is dependent upon the temporal creativity, is truly consequent upon the world. It therefore inherits from the world's temporality, though not contributing to the world's temporality. But just here is the second sense requiring God's relationship to time. God does not contribute to the world's temporality by any passage into pastness, but does surely contribute to the world in the superjective nature of a dynamic actuality. God's own feeling for the temporal world's future so influences that future that God becomes the ground of the successiveness which does occur, particularly if, as we have suggested, it is God's appetition toward a particular way of harmonizing a temporal past which evokes the occasion which utilizes that appetition as its initial aim. In this case, the temporal world depends for its very nature as process upon the satisfaction of God—this is its mode of novelty. This leads to a unique contrast whereby God, by virtue of nontemporality, is able to ground the temporality of the world. Given the relatedness of time and space, God is likewise the ground of the manner in which occasions realize spatial dimensions in their atomization of extensiveness.

If God is nontemporal and nonspatial, but is the ground of both qualities, then God must transcend by way of inclusion all manifestations of both qualities. In a sense, Whitehead implies this by noting that there is no metaphysical ultimacy concerning any particular way of atomizing the extensive continuum. What is ultimate, is the relatedness which allows the continuum. God, as well as all finite occasions, must express this relatedness. But the particularities of space and time are accidental.

The three dimensions of space form an additional fact about the physical occasions. Indeed, the sheer dimensionality of space, apart from the precise number of dimensions, is such an additional fact, not involved in the mere notion of extension. Also, the seriality of time, unique or multiple, cannot be derived from the sole notion of extension (PR 289).

Therefore, there could be other epochs which exhibit space/time relations different from those which we know. But God, as the everlastingly concrescent entity, must be related to the occasions of every epoch, and hence transcends the characteristics of any one. God is able to include all modes of space and time through the prehension of occasions which contribute the experience of such qualities to the divine nature, but God, being everlasting, is unlimited by any spatial/temporal necessities. God includes but transcends these qualities.[7]

I have referred to the fluency of God's concrescence, but this fluency is not a repetition of the epochal time of transition. The use of the word "dynamic" relative to God's harmony is intended to convey the difference between God's fluency and the givenness of epochal time, but this must be expanded.

If God prehended entities so that their "counterpart in God" simply repeated their occurrence in the world, albeit in a transformed way, then God's nature would demonstrate epochal time even though God would not add to it. Containing the counterpart in its givenness, there would then be the same transition of entities in God which perforce requires the passing mark of the space/time continuum. But Whitehead indicates that occasions are everlastingly in God in their immediacy, and that they are there not temporal but transformed into a "living, ever-present fact." He further allows the conclusion that in God's nature, the immediacies of many occasions are bound together in the immediacy of God through the unity of God's subjective aim. This aim, like the aim of every entity, is indivisible and constitutes the ultimate oneness of the divine nature. Further, this aim is but the exemplification of God's satisfaction, everlastingly enjoying a dynamic concreteness.

Whitehead states that every occasion is taken into the unity of God, that "this prehension into God of each creature is directed with the subjective aim, and clothed with the subjective form, wholly derivative from his all-inclusive primordial valuation" (PR 345). Consequently, the immediacy of each prehended occasion participates in the adventures of the eternal vision of God. United with God's primordial satisfaction, the occasions participate everlastingly in the exemplification of that satisfaction. They have become a part of the pattern which is the harmony of God. Insofar as there is successiveness in the concrescence of God through the "multiple unifications of the universe," each succeeding unification affects the entire pattern in which all participate.[8] By virtue of the unity of God and the present-ness required of all portions of an actual entity to itself, there is no "past" immediacy within God which is excluded from the enjoyment of the present unification. There is successiveness in God, but not seriality: the "past" enjoys the effects of the newly incorporated "present," just as that "present" enjoys the effect of the "past"— for all, indeed, are present in God's everlastingness. Each is a living participant in God's subjective form, which mediates the whole to each part. All are present in the presence of God. In place of an internal epochal measurement of time, there is fluent unity of being which increasingly intensifies because of the continuous expansion of the divine nature.

There are problems to be raised concerning this description as it relates to some of the principles of the theory of relativity. For instance, we have portrayed God as prehending every occasion upon its completion in such a way that the occasion is conformed to the primordial vision. Since complete occasions occur in different time frames, does God prehend them in some absolute sequence, which becomes an absolute "cosmic time"? Our denial of strict seriality within the consequent nature mitigates against this. Since God is not epochal, it is hard to understand the divine prehensions as establishing some ultimate epochal measurement. But further, there is the sense in which the relativity of time must be taken seriously as a feature of the temporal world. God's prehension of occasions is not in terms of their sequence, but in terms of their completion. It is we who mark out the various sequences. In the sense that each occasion in its immediacy perceives itself within a particular time frame, and that the occasion's immediacy is prehended and preserved in God, there is most certainly a sense in which God understands the varied time frames which do obtain. God experiences these derivatively, however, and transforms these experiences in conformation to the divine nature. Participating in God's nature, finite occasions transcend their temporality in the manner already discussed. God grounds all times, includes all times, and transcends all times. Therefore, God cannot contribute any one absolute sequence which could be understood as a standard cosmic time.

If God is nontemporal and transcends time, does God know times which are future relative to the world? Since the primordial nature is the eternal envisagement of all potentiality, can God know that potentiality as if it were actual? Given the kind of understanding we have outlined, it does not appear that there is either necessity or reason for God to know that which has not occurred beyond anticipatory feelings. On the contrary, since God's concrescence is the converse of the occasion's, moving from a simple determinacy to a "multiplicity of elements with individual self-realization" in "multiple unifications of the universe,"[9] it would be inconsistent for God to know an event prior to its occurrence. God's aim is qualitative, not designative of just what will be molded to that quality. The only real requirement is that the future, when it occurs, will be conformable to God's aim, but this is just what has been eternally assured in God's primordial satisfaction. God, knowing all potentiality, has valued a quality of existence which would work toward the enhancement of any conceivable actuality. But which potentialities will be selected by finite, temporal occasions await the decisions of such occasions. Until such decisions take place, there may be probabilities but not certainties with regard to what those decisions will be. The occasion retains its privacy within its own concrescent decisions.

The foreknowledge of God which is implied in the eternal vision is that no matter what an occasion may decide to become, the occasion will benefit from and contribute to the great harmony of God's divine satisfaction. Thus there is no reason for the presentness of God, in everlasting immediacy, to surpass the "isness" of actuality. Finite occasions contribute novelty in the sense of contributing specific actualities to God, even as God makes possibility and novelty available to the deciding occasions. God is both the condition and the outcome of creativity, the provider and the recipient of novelty, because of God's genuine openness toward actuality.

The effect of maintaining God's genuine openness toward the actualities of the temporal future is to underscore the responsive nature of God. God reaches toward the world both as it is and as it can be. The creativity of the world is accepted by God into the divine nature in a mutual enrichment of God and world. The world, which in its creativity is novel even to God, is made one with God through the truly responsive consequent nature. To the world, God as such an actual entity is truly "God for us"—and yet the world is equally for God. In the rhythmic responsiveness which is integral to the concept of God as an actual entity, the world moves toward its redemptive completion in God, adding thereby to the completion of God. And the reality in heaven passes back into the world in everlasting process.

Conclusion:
The End of Evil

Our journey has taken us through initial explorations into two formulations of the root of evil, freedom and finitude. For both Augustine and Leibniz, the issue was not only to understand the root problem of evil but to formulate powerful visions depicting the end of evil. For Augustine, this end involved a balancing of the cosmos in a perfect harmony, which depended upon an eternal punishment of those who marred the glory of God's creation, whether angelic or human. For Leibniz, the end was as ambiguous as the source. For all of his attempt to reformulate an argument that the freedom of the will created the problem of evil, his actual development indicated the problem of finitude. His expression of evil's end likewise has a share of ambiguity, for those violators of God's order will indeed receive punishment, and this punishment will be meted out in a City of God, akin to Augustine's vision. But unlike Augustine, Leibniz saw no separation of the damned and the redeemed, but rather envisioned them together in the City which is finally the preenvisioned harmony of God.

Kant, with his emphasis on the will, postulated a realm of immortality which would finally yield the happiness which should be attendant upon the moral will. He too visualized a City which was a kingdom of ends, and an ethical commonwealth where there would at last be a union of hearts. This City was the earthly goal of human existence, but the implications remain, as in Augustine and Leibniz, of an immortal City.

Schleiermacher, Hegel, and Nietzsche variously expressed the problem of evil in terms of finitude, and each gave his own variation on the precise nature of evil's effects and the envisioned resolution to evil's ills. Whether in a completion to all existence through the incarnate Redeemer, as in Schleiermacher, or through an ultimate realization of Absolute Spirit in and through human self-conscious-

153

ness, as in Hegel, or in the darker projections of Nietzsche's "amor fati!" and an eternal recurrence, each posed the hope of evil's end.

With such a legacy, a process theologian must continue the journey by utilizing the "both/and" nature of process thought. Both freedom and finitude qualify a process world, and evil is related to both, and conditioned by both. Evil—or the destruction of well-being in a variety of modes—follows from the fragility of interdependent existence, where the structure of internal relationships involves all existence in vulnerability. Within this vulnerability, the exercise of freedom has multiple effects, some of which will be inevitably experienced as contributing to well-being from a particular standpoint, but as detracting from or destroying well-being from another. There is a fundamental ambiguity to existence, with good and evil interwoven.

The ambiguity is intensified since the very structure which yields evil is precisely the structure which yields redemption. The vulnerability which forms the fragility of existence is the means for creating not only the richness of existence, but the very reality of existence. To exist is to be involved in internal relationships, open to and vulnerable to the energies of the past, and affecting the reality of the future. There is dependence upon the past and responsibility toward the future, and in this web of relationality, both good and evil find ambiguous expression.

In the process analysis, God, also, must be portrayed as involved in the relational structure of existence. God, as well as the world, is internally affected by that which is other; God, as well as the world, has an effect on the ongoing reality of temporal existence. Insofar as God is everlastingly one, then God everlastingly receives the world into the divine nature, transforming and unifying the world within the richness of the primordial vision. Consequent upon this process, God offers back to the world possibilities for its own transformation. These possibilities reflect the divine image insofar as they lead the world toward a rich diversity of communities of well-being, related to one another in harmony and peace. The possibilities reflect the world insofar as they are adapted to what is really possible in any locus. The dual reflection of God and the world in the possibilities means that what is actually possible will not be utopian, but it will be realizable, and if achieved will lead to new possibilities where the communal image of God will be even stronger. Whether these possibilities are actualized in time depends upon the free response of the world. Thus the end of evil is its continuous transformation in God beyond all history, which then provides possibilities for particular transformations in time. Within the finitude of time, there can be neither full nor final perfection, and every good must look to its own transformation.

This vision, like so many in our history, expresses the haunting hope of a "City not made with hands, eternal in the heavens," and that City is the very reality of God. The City calls us to its reflection in the cities of time, so that history can mirror a reconciliation of things in a peace which works the well-being of earth and its inhabitants. Our freedom and our finitude paradoxically hinder the task, and yet, with the ever-present empowerment of God, make it possible.

The expression of the end of evil in this volume has been developed primarily in philosophical categories rather than theological categories, although theological suppositions and implications have been woven throughout the presentation. It is, then, a natural theology that is foundationally Christian.[1] It is built upon the assumption that God is a power for redemption of history's sorrows. It is a particular vision of the end of evil, developed from a particular Christian standpoint and, therefore, reflecting that standpoint.

The mentor of all process theologians and philosophers speaks better than any of us to the hazards of attempting to envision the end of evil—those shoals which cause our shipwrecks. Whitehead wrote in his own small gem, "Immortality":

Of course we are unable to conceive the experience of the Supreme Unity of Existence. But these are the human terms in which we can glimpse the origin of that drive towards limited ideals of perfection which haunts the Universe. This immortality of the World of Action, derived from its transformation in God's nature, is beyond our imagination to conceive. The various attempts at description are often shocking and profane. What does haunt our imagination is that the immediate facts of present action pass into permanent significance for the Universe. The insistent notion of Right and Wrong, Achievement and Failure, depends upon this background. Otherwise every activity is merely a passing whiff of insignificance.[2]

That which is beyond our imagination nonetheless infuses our lives with hope, and the vision which is here so feebly expressed will gladly yield to a more perfect knowledge of evil's end.

Notes

Chapter I

1. Augustine, *On True Religion*, Xii.23; see also *The City of God*, XXII14, and *Concerning the Nature of the Good*, VII.

2. I have explored the parallel between *City of God* and *Confessions* in great detail in "The Symbolic Structure of Augustine's *Confessions*," published in *The Journal of the American Academy of Religion*, L/3 (September 1982). This present chapter presupposes the results of that research.

3. Augustine, *City of God*, XIV.XI. The translation ued is from *Basic Writings of Saint Augustine*, Volume II, edited, with an introduction and notes by Whitney J. Oates (New York: Random House, 1948). Henceforth references to *City of God* will be cited as CG.

4. Augustine, *Confessions*, II.VI. The translation used is from *Basic Writings of Saint Augustine*, Volume I, edited, with an introduction and notes by Whitney J. Oates (New York: Random House, 1948). Henceforth references to *Confessions* will be cited as Con.

5. CG XIV.XIII.

6. *Con.* II.X.

7. CG XIII.XIV.

8. Augustine, *On the Free Choice of the Will*, III.XV. The translation used is that by Anna S. Benjamin and L. H. Hackstaff (Indianapolis: The Bobbs-Merrill Company, Inc., 1964). Henceforth references to *On the Free Choice of the Will* will be cited as FCW.

9. *Con.* VII.XVII.

10. *Con.* VIII.IX.

11. *Con.* VIII.XI, XII.

12. FCW III.XV.

157

13. *FWC* III.IX.

14. Finalism, however, was included in the notion of God as first cause insofar as the design of the universe entered into the need for the cause. The Deists, notably Voltaire, held to final causation in this sense; yet their use differed significantly from that of Leibniz. Their emphasis was on God as the cause of the design rather than the end of the design; origin was more important than future purpose.

15. See especially the articles on "Manichees," "Pauliciens," "Pyrrho," and "Zabarella" (E. A. Beller and M. DuP. Lee, Jr. [eds.], *Selections from Bale's Dictionary* [Princeton: Princeton University Press, 1952]).

16. Thus Liebniz writes, "Thus God alone (or the necessary Being) has this prerogative that he must necessarily exist, if He is possible. And as nothing can interfere with the possibility of that which involves no limits, no negation and consequently no contradiction, this (his possibility) is sufficient of itself to make known the existence of God a priori" (*Monadology*, sec. 45).

Five essays by G. W. Leibniz will be cited in this chapter: "Discourse on Metaphysics" and "Monadology" (henceforth *DM* and *M*, respectively) from *Discourse on Metaphysics, Correspondence with Arnauld, and Monadology*, trans. G. R. Montgomery (LaSalle: The Open Court Publishing Co., 1962); "On the Ultimate Origin of Things" and "Principles of Nature and Grace" (henceforth *UOT* and *PNG*, respectively) from *The Monadology and Other Philosophical Writings*, trans. R. Latta (London: Oxford University Press, 1951); and *Theodicy* (henceforth *T*), ed. D. Allen, trans. E. M. Huggard (Indianapolis: The Bobbs-Merrill Co., 1966).

17. See *DM*, sec. 1; *PNG*, sec. 9; *M*, sec. 48.

18. *PNG*, sec. 9. It should be pointed out that the interaction of the three attributes does not present a limitation; rather, it provides the means for the fullest actualization of each.

19. These are equivalent to efficient cause and final cause on the finite level.

20. See also *DM*, sec. 26.

21. Leibniz discusses this interaction primarily in terms of the body and soul, accounting for the unity of the person. But the interaction extends beyond this, of course, into the larger realm of nature as a whole. See *M*, sec 78; *PNG*, sec. 3; *Theodicy*, sec. 62. Strictly speaking, the interaction is not "built into nature" in view of a harmony. Rather, that variation of a particular nature is chosen for actualization which will itself help to produce the harmony. This is discussed at greater length in the issue of freedom which will follow.

22. *PNG*, sec. 3. This analogy applies to the realm of nature; insofar as the realm of grace is concerned, the metaphor changes to that of the City of God, where God is Monarch and Father. See *PNG*, sec. 15.

23. *UOT*, sec. 346; *Theodicy*, sec. 119; *M*, sec. 60. If one wholly knew any one thing, one would know all, and this indeed is divine knowledge.

24. Time and space are derivative notions, abstracted from the existence of monads.

25. M, sec. 55.

26. The problem is tacitly acknowledged in the following passage: "I have proved that free will is the proximate cause of the evil of guilt and consequently of the evil of punishment; although it is true that the original imperfection of creatures, which is already presented in the eternal ideas, is the first and most remote cause" (*Theodicy*, sec. 20).

27. DM, sec. 30.

28. *Theodicy*, secs. 410–17. The illustration used here is of Sextus, but the principle is identical with that of Judas used in *Discourse on Metaphysics*.

29. PNG, sec. 15.

30. DM, sec. 4.

31. For instance, note the contrast within DM, sec. 35 where Leibniz says both "[God] can, so to speak, enter into conversation and even into social relations by communicating to them in particular ways his feelings and his will so that they are able to know and love their benefactor," and also the qualifying "[God's] glory and our worship can add nothing to his satisfaction, the recognition of creatures being nothing but a consequence of his sovereign and perfect felicity and being far from contributing to it or from causing it even in part." The first quotation is echoed frequently throughout the work. For example, in sec. 36 he writes, "It is through this [the moral quality of God] that he humanizes himself, and that he is willing to suffer anthropologies, and that he enters into social relations with us, and this consideration is so dear to him. . . ." It is hard to see how both statements are reconciled, despite the attempt at mere qualification. I take the conflict to be a symptom of the unsuccessful struggle to retain Augustinian categories of immutability, even while accepting the different substratum of infinitude, with its quite different implications.

Chapter II

1. Immanuel Kant, *Religion Within the Limits of Reason Alone*, trans. T. M. Greene and H. H. Hudson (New York: Harper & Row, 1960). Henceforth referred to in this work as *RWLRA*.

2. *RWLRA*, Bk. I, Secs. I and II.

3. *RWLRA*, p. 45; cf. p. 57, where this capacity in the human soul bespeaks a supernatural origin.

4. Ibid., pp. 40, 55, 78, 123.

5. Ibid., p. 32.

6. Ibid., p. 54.

7. Ibid., p. 44.

8. Ibid. p. 54.

9. Cf. "General Observation" sections appended to Books I and IV, RWLRA.

10. RWLRA, p. 89.

11. Friedrich Schleiermacher, The Christian Faith, vols. I and II, ed. H. R. Mackintosh and J. S. Stewart (New York: Harper & Row, 1960).

12. Schleiermacher, I: 17. Interestingly, Jügen Moltmann develops a similar notion. It is given particularly clear expression in his article, "Hope and the Biomedical Future of Man," Hope and the Future of Man, ed. Ewert H. Cousins (Philadelphia: Fortress Press, 1972).

13. This is the explanation most frequently cited by Schleiermacher, but in his development it bears the deeper implications given above.

14. Schleiermacher, I: 391.

15. Ibid., p. 317.

16. The question of the actual application of this completion to the beings of the world is answered by Schleiermacher primarily in terms of the community of the church, receiving and spreading this effect pervasively in the world.

17. Schleiermacher, I: 199.

18. Ibid., pp. 15–18, 206.

19. Ibid., p. 16.

Chapter III

1. G.W.F. Hegel, The Christian Religion, ed. and trans. Peter C. Hodgson (Missoula: The Scholars Press, 1979), p. 131.

2. Ibid., p. 133; see also p. 140.

3. Ibid., p. 169

4. George R. Lucas, Jr., develops an interesting comparative study of the concept of freedom in Whitehead and in Hegel: Two Views of Freedom in Process Thought: A Study of Hegel and Whitehead (Missoula: Scholars Press, 1979).

5. See The Politics of Salvation: The Hegelian Idea of the State, by Paul Lakeland (Albany: State University of New York Press, 1984). The analogy between the state and the family is developed on pp. 24–29.

6. Hegel, The Christian Religion. p. 131.

7. Hegel's Philosophy of Mind, Being Part Three of the Encyclopaedia of the Philosophical Sciences (1830), trans. William Wallace, together with the Zusatze in Boumann's text (1845), trans. A. V. Miller (Oxford: Clarendon Press, 1971), p. 277 Zusatze.

8. Ibid., p. 564.

9. Hegel, The Christian Religion, see pp. 26–34.

10. Ibid., pp. 201–7.

11. Ibid., p. 209: ". . . this return and elevation to the right hand of God is only one side of the consummation of the third sphere. For this third sphere is the idea in its character as individuality, but in the first instance it portrays only a single individuality, the divine, universal individuality, individuality as it is in and for itself. One is all; once is always . . . individuality as being-for-self is this act of releasing the differentiated moments to free immediacy and independence . . . and is the return from others into itself. The individuality of the divine Idea . . . has many individuals confronting it and brings these back into the unity of Spirit, into the community, and therein exists as an actual, universal, self-consciousness."

12. Schopenhauer's *The World as Will and Idea* seems to pick up on such Hegelian sensitivities.

13. Hegel, *Philosophy of History*, trans. by J. Sibree (New York: P. F. Collier & Son, 1905), p. 66.

14. Hegel, *Encyclopaedia*, p. 209, *Zusatz*.

15. This is obviously from the linear perspective of history; a continuous intersection of finite-infinite throughout history offers different possibilities. There may be parallels between Hegel's formulations and those which are possible in a process eschatology.

16. F. Nietzxche, *The Will to Power*, ed. W. Kaufmann, trans. W. Kaufmann and R. J. Hollingdale (New York: Random House, Inc., 1967), fragment 12.

17. Feuerbach appears to be a particularly strong influence upon Nietzsche at this point; also Schopenhauer. Cf. F. Nietzsche, *The Will to Power*, fragments 17, 27, 30, 32.

18. See the discussion on nihilism between Danto and Schacht in *Nietzsche: A Collection of Critical Essays*, ed. R. Solomon (Garden City: Anchor Press, 1973).

19. F. Nietzsche, *The Gay Science*, translated, with commentary, by Walter Kaufmann (New York: Vintage Books, 1974), III.25, p. 181.

20. F. Nietzsche, *The Will to Power*, fragment 12 (A).

21. F. Nietzsche, *On the Genealogy of Morals*, trans. W. Kaufmann and R. J. Hollingdale (New York: Random House, Inc., 1967), p. 163.

22. Nietzsche, *The Will to Power*, fragment 25.

23. Ibid., fragment 1014.

24. Ibid., fragment 1031.

25. F. Nietzsche. *Thus Spake Zarathustra*, from *The Complete Works of Friedrich Nietzsche*, vol. 11, ed. Oscar Levy, trans. Thomas Common (New York: Russell & Russell, Inc., 1964).

26. Nietzsche evidently argued for the literalness of the doctrine of eternal recurrence—though not in the writings which he published, where it is presented in poetic or fanciful terms. Arthur Danto, "The Eternal Recurrence," *Nietzsche: A Collection of Critical Essays*, presents and discusses the unpublished arguments left by Nietzsche.

27. Nietzsche, *Thus Spake Zarathustra*, p. 168.

28. I have purposefully cast Nietzsche's *Ubermensch* into the feminine gender for two reasons. First, while Nietzsche, in his patriarchal society, most likely had males in mind (Frau Lou notwithstanding), it is the case that the German *Mensch* translates as human beings rather than as the more gender specific "men" or "women." Thus the application of the word to a woman is as appropriate as to a man. But second, and most important, the use of the feminine underscores the radical discontinuity Nietzsche envisaged for *Ubermensch*. Women have no recorded history in patriarchy; hence there is a sense in which their arrival into history is less an emergence than an eruption born of woman's own will. She storms history, taking it by force. There is thus an analogy between the woman of feminism and Nietzsche's *Ubermensch*.

29. Nietzsche, *The Will to Power*, fragment 486.

Chapter IV

1. The two major works by Alfred North Whitehead which will be used most frequently in this and the following chapters will be *Adventures of Ideas* (New York: The Free Press, 1967) and *Process and Reality*, corrected edition, ed. David Ray Griffin and Donald W. Sherburne (New York: The Free Press, 1978). When quoted in the texts or referred to in subsequent notes, the quotations will be identified by the initials *AI* or *PR* and the page number.

2. See also *PR*, p. 340: "The ultimate evil in the temporal world is deeper than any specific evil. It lies in the fact the past fades, that time is a 'perpetual perishing.' . . . The nature of evil is that the characters of things are mutually obstructive." This entire section (V.I.IV) deals with the elaboration of evil as the destruction which is involved in the transience of existence.

3. David Ray Griffin, in *God, Power, and Evil: A Process Theodicy* (Philadelphia: The Westminster Press, 1976), gives an extended discussion of evil as triviality and as discord, pp. 282–85. See also John B. Cobb, Jr., and David Griffin, *Process Theology: An Introductory Exposition* (Philadelphia: The Westminster Press, 1976), p. 70.

4. See Whitehead, *PR*, pp. 90–91, 223: "A new actuality may appear in the wrong society, amid which its claims to efficacy act mainly as inhibitions. Then a weary task is set for creative function, by an epoch of new creations to remove the inhibition. Insistence on birth at the wrong season is the trick of evil. In other words, the novel fact may throw back, inhibit, and delay. But the advance, when it does arrive, will be richer in content, more fully conditioned, more stable. For in its objective efficacy an actual entity can only inhibit by reason of its alternative positive contribution."

5. Virginia Lieson Brereton and Christa Ressmeyer Klein, "American Women in Ministry: A History of Protestant Beginning Points," in *Women of Spirit: Female Leadership in the Jewish and Christian Traditions*, ed. E. McLaughlin and R. Ruether (New York: Simon and Schuster, 1979), p. 312.

6. *AI*, p. 269.

7. Cf. *PR*, 223: "The categories governing the determinations of things are the reasons why there should be evil; and are also the reasons why, in the advance of the world, particular evil facts are finally transcended."

8. Thus David Ray Griffin argues in *God, Power, and Evil: A Process Theodicy* that while "the possibility of genuine evil is rooted in the metaphysical (i.e., necessary) characteristics of the world" (p. 276), the ultimate reason for evil lies within the freedom of the actual entity (see chapter 18, "A Process Theodicy"). Likewise, Barry L. Whitney in *Evil and the Process God* (New York and Toronto: The Edwin Mellen Press, 1985), claims that "a central feature of process theodicy is its defence of the free will solution" (p. 116). Insofar as evil is considered the result of the occasion's choice not to conform to the initial aim received from God, the position is valid. However, if evil is *also* "fading of the past" such that there is inevitably a loss of value within the very nature of things, and that evil resides in the inevitable conflict of values residing in finitude, then one must hold a balanced tension between evil as free choice and evil as entailed in the conditions of finitude. The tension is captured by Charles Birch and John B. Cobb, Jr., in their *The Liberation of Life* (Cambridge: Cambridge University Press, 1981), with the image of "the fall upward" (see pp. 117–22). Also, David R. Griffin's essay, "Creation out of Chaos and the Problem of Evil," in *Encountering Evil*, ed. Stephen T. Davis (Atlanta: John Knox Press, 1981), maintains a tension between finitude and freedom.

9. *AI*, p. 291.

10. A. N. Whitehead, "Mathematics and the Good," in *The Philosophy of Alfred North Whitehead*, ed. P. A. Schilpp (LaSalle: The Open Court Publishing Co., 1941), pp. 674–75.

11. *PR*, p. 25 (category of explanation xxi).

12. Nancy Frankenberry, in "Some Problems in Process Theodicy" (*Religious Studies* 17: 179–197), argues that process theologians fail to note the ambiguity and tragedy of life, and hence develop theodicies which deal with a world too neatly described in terms of the either-or dichotomies of light or darkness, coercion or persuasion, good or evil. I am in agreement with her concerning the fundamental ambiguity of existence, arguing subsequently that the structure of redemption is in fact the structure of evil as well.

13. David Ray Griffin and John B. Cobb, Jr., make a similar point in their distinction between the intrinsic value of an occasion and the instrumental value of an occasion. See *Process Theology: An Introductory Exposition*, p. 71.

14. W. Pannenberg's position that history's meaning can only be determined by its completion has analogies to the view expressed here.

15. A. N. Whitehead, *Religion in the Making* (Cleveland: The World Publishing Co., 1960), p. 94.

16. Schilpp, ed., *The Philosophy of . . .* , p. 670.

17. *AI*, p. 268.

18. See J. Goheen's essay, "Whitehead's Theory of Value," in *The Philosophy of . . .* , ed. P. A. Schilpp. Goheen finds an inconsistency with reference to the definitive understanding of the Good, since, on the one hand, Whitehead values the definite pattern which is attained in the unity of the satisfaction of an entity, and on the other hand, he values the discord which indicates a striving for, rather than attainment of, the pattern. The position does not seem contradictory to me owing to the dynamism of the process which occurs both microcosmically in the occasion, and macrocosmically in the universe. The attainment of the unity of pattern in the occasion is simultaneously the presentation of new data, and inevitably discord, in the universe as a whole. Thus the two values Goheen notes, while distinctly two values in the abstraction of analysis, are really one value in two perspectives in actuality. It is precisely this double-sidedness of the value which accounts for process itself. Given this understanding, it seems to me that Whitehead is justified in referring to the totality of the harmony of the universe, which after all incorporates many harmonies, as the complex pattern of the Good.

19. *AI*, pp. 291, 295.

20. This metaphysical principle is relevant to the search for "hidden histories" which marks the transition of a suppressed group into historical dialogue with the dominant group, and within itself. Since negative prehensions bear the "scars of their birth" (*PR* 226), recorded history bears the trace of that which it has excluded. By searching history with a "hermeneutics of suspicion," it is possible to uncover the effect of the stories which were not explicitly told.

21. Lewis S. Ford's remarkable volume, *The Emergence of Whitehead's Metaphysics, 1925-1929* (Albany: State University of New York Press, 1984), details Whitehead's progressive development of an understanding of God.

22. There is some ambiguity in Kant's position. In some respects, he portrays radical evil as being precisely a Pelagian position, with every human capable of actualizing the good rather than the evil throughout life. But in other respects, the undeveloped potentiality for the moral law which is given to human nature entails that one's first actions are without recourse to the moral law, in which case there would seem to be an inevitability to evil.

23. See George R. Lucas, Jr., *Two Views of Freedom in Process Thought: A Study of Hegel and Whitehead* (Missula, Montana: The Scholars Press, 1979), and *Hegel and Whitehead: Contemporary Perspectives on Systematic Philosophy*, ed. George R. Lucas, Jr. (Albany: State University of New York Press, 1986).

24. For another study of the relation between Whitehead and Nietzsche, see "Whitehead and Nietzsche: Overcoming the Evil of Time," by Strachan Donnelley (*Process Studies* 12/1, Spring 1982).

Chapter V

1. In *God, Power, and Evil: A Process Theodicy*, David R. Griffin poses the issue that "the question is not how we explain evil—for by definition it is an absurdity, and hence inexplicable—but how we overcome it" (p. 16). He rejects this line of reasoning on the grounds that inadequate conceptions of evil contribute to the suffering of evil, and because of the theoretical implications of every question concerning evil. In response, I argue that many of the questions concerning the cause of evil are in fact quests for a meaning despite evil which would itself become an answer of sorts to the problem—the loss of meaning is the problem, and a posited rationality to the evil becomes the redemptive answer. Thus even the theodical question is a quest not simply for the source of evil but for the end of evil.

2. Most process theologians have held that objective immortality—the continuing effectiveness of the occasion in the ongoing world, and the everlasting (albeit nonsubjective) effectiveness of the occasion in God is either sufficient to answer the problem of evil or the only nonhistorical answer possible. The most cogent development of this theme is perhaps given in Schubert Ogden's article, "The Meaning of Christian Hope," *Union Seminary Quarterly Review* 30 (1975): 153–64. My answer to him in "The Question of Immortality," *Journal of Religion* 57/3 (July 1977): 288–306, argues that objective immortality is sufficient only for those who have lived moderately fortunate lives; for those who have been broken by evil, only subjective immortality can provide a sufficient redemption.

Arguments for subjective immortality have been discussed with varying degrees of tentativeness in the following works: Marjorie Suchocki, *The Correlation Between God and Evil*, unpublished Ph.D. dissertation and precursor to this present volume (Claremont, 1974); Tyron Inbody, "Process Theology and Personal Survival," *The Iliff Review* 31 (1974): 31–42 (Inbody argues for objective immortality, but suggests that personal survival might also be possible); David Ray Griffin, "The Possibility of Subjective Immortality in the philosophy of Whitehead," *The Modern Schoolman* 53 (1975): 342-360 (Griffin suggests that the body which currently supports the soul might be replaced with a different type of supportive society in a life beyond physical death); John B. Cobb, Jr. *Christ in a Pluralistic Age* (Philadelphia: The Westminster Press, 1975), chapter 16 (he looks toward a new unity wherein matter is no longer separated but is drawn into an inclusive whole); Lewis S. Ford and Marjorie Suchocki, "A Whiteheadian

Reflection on Immortality," *Process Studies* 7/1 (Spring 1977): 1–13; Marjorie Suchocki, "The Question of Immortality," *Journal of Religion* 57/3 (July 1977) (this treatment argues that God prehends the entirety of the satisfaction, the entirety of the occasion's past actual world, and therefore has the materials for the reenactment of the concrescent immediacy); Lewis S. Ford, *The Lure of God* (Philadelphia: Fortress Press, 1978), chapter 8 (Ford's admitted ambiguity concerning subjective immortality is evident in this volume—his lively mind continues to probe both sides of the question; in this work and in subsequent discussions, he has serious doubts concerning the viability of the concept); Charles Hartshorne, "Three Responses to Neville's *Creativity and God*," *Process Studies* 10/3–4 (Fall-Winter 1980): 93–97; Marjorie Suchocki, *God-Christ-Church: A Practical Guide to Process Theology* (New York: Crosssroad Publishing Company, 1982), chapter 17; and Joseph Bracken, *The Triune Symbol: Persons, Process, and Community* (Lanham: University Press of America, 1985), chapter 7 (Bracken argues for a communal immortality on the basis of his uniquely redeveloped doctrines of the trinity).

Of the above, the position of Charles Hartshorne is closest to this present work. He argues, as do I, that immediacy is contained in the satisfaction of an entity, that God prehends the fullness of the satisfaction, and therefore that God retains the immediacy of the satisfaction. In contrast to me, however, he does not understand the immediacy to undergo transformation; it is retained as the living memory of God. However, since he interprets God to be a series of occasions rather than a single everlasting entity, it seems to me that he could allow some form of transformation. If God is a series, then God's living memory is mediated to the divine presence through con-tinuously successive prehensions of God's own past. Since the same occasion cannot be prehended twice, would not the reprehensions through the divine succession introduce some mode of novelty into the living memory, and hence transformation?

3. Whitehead's own direct treatment of immortality is given in his essay, "Immortality," contained in *The Philosophy of Alfred North Whitehead*, ed. Paul Arthur Schilpp (LaSalle: Open Court, 1941 and 1951): 682–700. While he purports to be treating "the immortality of human beings" (p. 683), he is intentionally vague as to details. This vagueness is based upon the limited perspectives allowed in a universe where even "common sense" notions depend upon "our relation to the infinity of the Universe" (p. 699). Within this qualification, he contrasts the World of Fact (finitude) with the World of Value (infinitude), arguing (much as does Hegel) that each must be present in and to the other. His most concrete statements concerning immortality are that "the World of Value exhibits the essential unification of the Universe. Thus while it exhibits the immortal side of the many persons, it also involves the unification of personality. This is the concept of God" (p. 694). Later on the same page he writes that God "is the unification of the multiple personalities received from the Active World." Whitehead

does not expand upon these notions; I hope to do so in this and the following chapters.

4. *PR*, pp. 22–26 (categories iv, vi, vii, xxiv). The quotation is from category iv.

5. Ibid., p. 116.

6. In *Creativity and God: A Challenge to Process Theology*, Robert C. Neville raises the question of decision with regard to the Category of the Ultimate. That is, Whitehead's ontological principle demands that the reason for things be accounted for through an actual entity, which is itself a process of decision. What "decision" then accounts for the metaphysical categories which God as well as every occasion exemplifies? What accounts for the "ultimacy" of the Category of the Ultimate? If the categories simply "are," is there not an arbitrariness in the system? Neville then proposes a different concept of God which identifies God with creativity, beyond being, but decisive. The metaphysical structure of all created existence is the first created fact, a result of the sheer decisiveness of the transcendent reality. At issue is the ontological status of a description of reality. That is, if the "Category of the Ultimate" and the various attendant categories are philosophic generalizations drawn from the analysis of observed fact, why must the generalization be accounted for by something other than that which generates it? Would this not be a reification of the generalization tantamount to the fallacy of misplaced concreteness? Neville might respond that this begs the question, that actuality is an instantiation of something which itself must be explained. In order to avoid infinite regress, there must be a transcendent element beyond the system, accounting for the system as system. However, would not such transcendence be in principle unknowable if it did not participate in the categories of existence? ". . . there is an essence to the universe which forbids relationships beyond itself, as a violation of its rationality," wrote Whitehead (PR 4). We inescapably describe our realities from their midst; there are no skyhooks to take us beyond the universe. Even speculative imagination providing the negation of fanciful contrast must finally have recourse to the stories told for verification of the insight thus gained.

7. Lewis S. Ford reevisions transitional creativity in such a way that it would seem to belong entirely to God. In "The Divine Activity of the Future" (*Process Studies* 11/3, Fall 1981) he constructs an ingenious argument to the effect that God is future rather than contemporary relative to every actual occasion. God prehends each occasion upon its completion, and unifies all prehensions in as many ways as they can possibly be unified and so far as they can possibly be unified within the divine nature. However, the divine unification can proceed just so far and then must stop, since God cannot provide the "final determinate unity of that particular multiplicity" (p. 172). God then transfers this portion of the unification to the present, whereupon the finite occasion completes the process as its own self-creative present. Such a revision of Whitehead's system seems to indicate that only

God possesses transitional creativity relative to the world, and that occasions do not prehend at all, they simply inherit an already begun unification from God.

8. *PR*, p. 349.

9. *PR*, p. 225: "But, of course, there is no meaning to 'creativity' apart from its 'creatures,' and no meaning to 'God' apart from the 'creativity' and the 'temporal creatures,' and no meaning to the 'temporal creatures' apart from 'creativity' and 'God.' " This is a restatement of the Category of the Ultimate (one, many, and creativity).

10. This does not negate the central Whiteheadian insight tht effects produce themselves from their causes. An active rather than passive presentation of alternatives, multiplied by the many occasions of a past actual world, still requires that the nascent occasion selectively contrast and compare those alternatives. Thus the occasion is still *causa sui*, and responsible for its own creative unification of its past.

11. Lewis S. Ford points out to me that givenness *is* givingness if we consider concrescent creativity, wherein each phase gives way to the next.

12. I observed in note 2 that Hartshorne argues a position similar to my own with regard to immediacy being retained in an occasion's satisfaction. Robert C. Neville, in *Creativity and God: A Challenge to Process Theism* (New York: The Seabury Press, 1980) and in "Concerning Creativity and God: A Response" (*Process Studies* 11/1, Spring 1981), refutes this position. He argues that "becoming cannot be a term in a relation so as to be contained in a subsequent prehension because it has no existence except in its satisfaction, which is no longer becoming" (PS 11/1: 2). Neville assumes that the objectivity of a prehension is determined by the satisfaction itself; becoming yields definiteness, and only definiteness may be prehended. I contend that it is not definiteness which dissolves the immediacy, but division. To divide the occasion, which is inescapably whole, is to lose the immediacy which is constituted by precisely that whole. Further, the satisfaction retains the immediacy since the satisfaction is an integral portion of the occasion itself, and the occasion is genetically indivisible. The satisfaction is not "outside" the occasion, but part of the occasion. Genetic "time" is holistic, such that the occasion in and for itself is the result together with its becoming. Only transitional time yields the linearity of discreteness.

13. *PR*, p. 25 (categories of explanation xxi, xxii)

14. The initial aim will be discussed in detail in chapter VII, "The Structure of Temporal Redemption."

15. *PR*, p. 348.

15. Ibid., p. 345, with reference to the primordial nature. However, the consequent nature is the manifestation in concrete form of the primordial nature, and by inference, is also devoid of negative prehensions.

17. Richard Rorty, in "Matter and Event" (*Explorations in Whitehead's Philosophy*, ed., L. S. Ford and G. L. Kline [New York: Fordham University Press, 1983]), elaborates upon Whitehead's basic distinction

between repeatable universals and unrepeatable particularities. That which has external relations is definite and repeatable; it is objectifiable as a complex eternal object. However, the decisively concrescent subject of internal relations is not yet definite, and not repeatable. The difference is between the past and the present. Lewis S. Ford raises the question that if God prehends the occasion's subjective immediacy, is there not a violation of the very advance which Whitehead achieved through his definite/decisive distinction relative to universals and particulars? I suggest that the distinction, which is essentially one of time, is retained vis-à-vis temporal reality, which is precisely where the issue lies. However, just as the objective prehensions ensure time for the finite order, the subjective prehensions ensure process for the divine order. Rorty notes that the occasion as past could be described as one extremely complex eternal object (p. 95). Given this, one would almost have to posit that God prehends the immediacy in order to introduce novelty into God at all. God already contains through the primordial envisagement all eternal objects, complex and simple. Thus if God only prehends the objectivity of the occasion, there is not much point in the prehension: nothing is added, and God becomes static. But this is not the case; the world contributes novelty to God. I maintain that in all respects God and the occasion are reversals of each other: finite occasions prehend occasions objectively (thus satisfying Rorty's argument and the temporal order), and God prehends occasions subjectively (thus contributing novelty and process to God, allowing the divine concrescence). This matter of the reversal will be dealt with more fully in Chapter VII.

18. Cf. *PR*, pp. 88, 89, 105.
19. Ibid., p. 47.
20. *AI*, pp. 194–95.
21. *PR*, pp. 343, 345.

Chapter VI

1. The "Inferno" of Dante's *Divine Comedy* recounts the story of Paolo and Francesca, locked in everlasting embrace as punishment for their illicit love. This is in the second circle of Hell, reserved for carnal offenders. Pleasure endured in unalleviated sameness is no longer pleasure, but torment.

2. This constitutes my basic difference with Hartshorne, who maintains that God receives the subjective immediacy of the occasion, but does not develop the effects of God's concrescence on the occasion itself.

3. *PR*, p. 348: "Creation achieves the reconciliation of permanence and flux when it has reached its final term which is everlastingness—the Apotheosis of the World." Clearly, in Whitehead, the occasion becomes a

participant in God's own nature, where it experiences what in theological terms is called redemption. See also *PR.*, Part V, Section VI.

4. David Griffin has suggested the possibility of a continuing seriality for occasions in God in "The Possibility of Subjective Immortality in the Philosophy of Whitehead," *The Modern Schoolman* 53 (1975): 342–60. The problem, however, is that it would require separate concrescences within the one concrescence of God. If such a thing were conceivable, there would be the additional problem of new initial aims and the concrescing freedom to deviate from the aim, which is one ground of evil. In that case, how would existence in God be an advance over finitude? Would it not be a repetition of finitude?

5. *AI*, pp.259–60.

6. There is a long history in Whiteheadian scholarship of interpretations concerning personal identity, and an equally long history of challenges to those interpretations. The problem has to do with how one extends Whitehead's rather incomplete analysis. For Whitehead, personal identity is the sense by which we "objectify the occasions of our own past with peculiar completeness in our immediate present" (PR 161), but this "peculiar completeness" in not given any systematic development. His theory has been criticized as leading to personal identity as no more than a congery of separate occasions with no real connection explaining personal order. One possible way to deal with the problem is to note that consciousness is a subjective form involved in later phases of concrescence (PR 162). Consciousness as subjective form also qualifies satisfaction, but not as *self-consciousness*—"No actual entity can be conscious of its own satisfaction; for such knowledge would be a component in the process, and would thereby alter the satisfaction" (PR 85). This indicates that the mode of consciousness in satisfaction relates only to the actual experience of unification, not reflection on that experience. And yet we, in our personhood, experience self-consciousness. My suggestion is that the "peculiar completeness" of prehension entailed in personhood is prehension of the consciousness of the immediate past. Our reflective consciousness is of the immediately past consciousness, not of the present. Given the rapidity of succession, consciousness would then give the illusion of continuity, whereas in actuality, it would be a linkage successively obtained—but it would account for identity. It would mean that self-consciousness is always one step behind itself. The "dejavu's" of our experience would be based on the reality that we *had* already gone through that experience; it would be the occasional slip-up of "catching-up" with ourselves.

7. I have given a more theologically oriented discussion of judgment as heaven or hell in Chapter XVII of *God-Christ-Church: A Practical Guide to Process Theology*.

8. Whitehead writes that "the revolts of destructive evil, purely self-regarding, are dismissed into their triviality of merely individual facts" (PR) 346), and on this basis some might argue that there is not universal

redemption, but selective redemption in Whitehead's enigmatic vision. But in the same passage, Whitehead also writes that "the consequent nature of God is his judgment upon the world. He saves the world as it passes into the immediacy of his own life. It is the judgment of a tenderness which loses nothing that can be saved. It is also the judgment of a wisdom which uses what in the temporal world is mere wreckage" (PR 346). I have extended this to indicate that while the process of redemption is the same for all occasions in God, the qualitative results of redemption reflect the everlastingly retained finite satisfaction. The unity of God is a complex diversity. The biblical parallel would be the apostle Paul's metaphor in I Corinthians 15 that "star differs from star in glory."

Chapter VII

1. The ability of an occasion to receive an initial aim from God has been a matter of some controversy in process thought. The problem involves Whitehead's dictum that contemporaries cannot prehend one another; this, in turn, is essential to the relativity theory of time. The dominant way of dealing with the problem was through Charles Hartshorne's revision, whereby God is not considered to be an actual entity, as in Whitehead, but as a series of actual entities. John B. Cobb, Jr., followed Hartshorne in this move, as did most process philosophers (William Christian and Lewis S. Ford are notable exceptions). On this theory, each finite occasion prehends God's immediately past satisfaction, and hence the problem of contemporary prehension is avoided. My own position is that the reversal of poles in God entails a primordial satisfaction, and, therefore, constitutes a definiteness whereby God can be prehended without violating the categories. This position is expanded in "The Metaphysical Ground of the Whiteheadian God," *Process Studies* 5/4 (Winter 1975). The present work builds upon the earlier article, but develops it further. Finally, while I think the societal view effectively eliminates the primordial nature, it also entails the problem that the number of unifications required in a series in order to match every single finite concrescence whatsoever defy probability. Whitehead's view of God as a single actual entity, understood as the reversal of finite dynamics, seems a simpler way to address the problem.

2. PR, p. 32: "Thus God has immortality in respect to his primordial nature and his consequent nature."

3. Perhaps the most haunting implications of the effectiveness of the consequent nature are contained in the enigmatic "Immortality" (in *The Philosophy of Alfred North Whitehead*, ed. P. Schilpp [LaSalle: Open Court, 1941/1951]). Whitehead speaks of the "World of Value (God) and the

"World of Fact" (also called World of Origination, of Activity, and Creative World, all of which signify finitude) as abstractions if considered in separation from one another, since the reality is that each requires the other, and exhibits the impress of the other. God is described as the "unification of the multiple personalities received from the Active World" (p. 694), which leads to "the coordination of all possibility for entry into the active World of Fact" (p. 696). Finally, the "origin of that drive towards limited ideals of perfection" (a description of the initial aim) is "derived from its [the world's] transformation in God's nature" (p. 698). In this essay, Whitehead is not using the terminology of primordial and consequent for the nature of God, but it is clear that the effect of God on the world derives from the transformation of the now-immortal world through the power or God's own vision of Harmony.

4. *AI*, Part IV.

5. Cf. "Immortality," cited above; "The two worlds of Value and of Action are bound together in the life of the Universe, so that the immortal factor of Value enters into the active creation of temporal fact" (p. 687).

6. Whitehead is often read as requiring actualization of the vision only in the world; "Immortality" (and sections of *PR*) makes clear that through the means of immortality, the actualization refers to the life of God as well.

7. In "Immortality," this transformation refers primarily to human personalities, such that God is the "unification of the multiple personalities received from the Active World" (p. 694); also, God "receives into its unity the scattered effectiveness of realized activities, transformed by the supremacy of its own ideals" (p. 698).

8. Cf. the closing paragraph of Section XVII, "immortality," (p. 698).

9. This would be through the subjective form of God, which provides the interconnectedness of every prehension within the divine concrescence; Whitehead calls this the "mutuality of subjective form."

10. God does not prehend occasions serially, one after another—God simply prehends each occasion upon its completion. The serial time marked by this completion is relevant only to the finite entities which inherit from the occasion; it is not relevant to God's prehension. God's time is the internal time of concrescence, as will be discussed in Chapter VIII.

11. Cf. *PR*, p. 223.

12. *Process Studies* 15/4 (Winter 1986), ed. George Allan, is a special issue on social philosophy. Joseph A. Bracken, Randall C. Morris, and Paul Lakeland present diverse opinions on the analogical possibilities between concrescence and forms of civic existence. I follow Bracken in preferring to deal with an analogy drawn from personal existence rather than from the actual occasion on the basis that as societies increase in complexity, the organization is less controlled. An actual occasion has total control of itself within its boundaries; a society does not. Therefore there are more parallels between the societal organization of human persons and the larger societies in which we live.

13. However, ecclesiology has not been of prime interest to process theologians. The most specific work done in this area has been by Bernard Lee, *The Becoming of the Church: A Process Theology of the Structure of Christian Experience* (New York: The Paulist Press, 1974). By and large, process theologians dealing with the community focus their efforts on society as a whole, particularly insofar as process theology is aligned with liberation and political theology. Among the relevant works are: Schubert M. Ogden, *Faith and Freedom* (Nashville: Abingdon, 1979); Delwin Brown, *To Set at Liberty: Christian Faith and Human Freedom* (Maryknoll: Orbis Books, 1981); John B. Cobb, Jr., *Process Theology as Political Theology* (Philadelphia: Westminster Press, 1982); see also *Process Studies* 14/2 (Summer 1985), a special issue on Liberation Theology edited by Joseph A. Bracken, S.J.

14. There is an essential element of ideological pluralism built into the very notion of communities in process thought. The supposition is that the total human community is enriched not by ideological uniformity but by the particularity of diversities. John B. Cobb, Jr. addresses the reality of ideological diversity in "Buddhist Emptiness and the Christian God," *Journal of the American Academy of Religion* 45/1 (1977): 11-25 and in *Beyond Dialogue: Toward a Mutual Transformation of Christianity and Buddhism* (Philadelphia: Fortress Press, 1982).

15. Walter Rauschenbusch, *A Theology for the Social Gospel* (Nashville: Abingdon, 1978).

Chapter VIII

1. *PR*, p. 21.

2. For example, see *PR*, pp. 36 and 348. While on p. 224 Whitehead introduces the notion that an occasion "in one sense originates from its mental pole, analogously to God himself," he then must qualify this by noting that its initial conceptuality nevertheless derives from the prehension of God. Since God is an actual entity, the prehension is physical, defined as "prehensions whose data involve actual entities" (p. 23). Therefore, the distinction of the reversal holds: God and the occasions exhibit the same metaphysical principles, but conversely to each other.

3. *PR*, pp. 149–50.

4. "Beginning" must be considered in the sense of primordial, and not in the sense whereby God comes into existence from nothingness. Primordially considered, God is eternal.

5. Whitehead states that the primordial nature of God is not conscious, and that consciousness is achieved through the integration of the physical and mental feelings. But since God is an actual entity, and not simply a

primordial nature, God satisfies the requirements of consciousness: God is always consequent as well as always primordial, and the consequent nature is always interacting with the primordial.

6. *PR*, pp. 87–88.

7. An analogous situation obtains with negative prehensions. God is devoid of negative prehensions, and prehends all occasions in their entirety. But the occasions which are prehended have themselves been constituted through negative as well as positive prehensions. Insofar as God thoroughly knows the occasion, the negative prehensions are known as well. But God can be said to know them derivatively, or indirectly, since God does not negatively prehend occasions. Even so with time: God is not in time, but the occasions prehended have known time. Insofar as God knows the occasions, God knows time as well. But time does not occur within the divine nature in the same epochal sense in which it occurs through the world.

8. Cf. "Immortality."

9. *PR*, pp. 350 and 349, respectively.

Conclusion

1. John B. Cobb, Jr., in *A Christian Natural Theology*. (Philadelphia: The Westminster Press, 1965), laid the foundation for this task.

2. Alfred North Whitehead, "Immortality," in *Library of Living Philosophers*, vol. III: *The Philosophy of Alfred North Whitehead*, ed. Paul A. Schilpp (Chicago: Northwestern University, 1941), p. 698.

Glossary
of
Process Terms*

Actual Entity. Each unit of process is called an actual entity; it is a drop of experience that comes into existence through the creative process of concrescence. Actual entities are the "final real things of which the world is made up." They are the building blocks that, through an essential interconnectedness, make up the composite world of rocks, trees, and people.

Actual Occasion. This phrase is almost a synonym for actual entity, with the one distinction that the world occasion implies a locus in the spatio-temporal extensiveness of the universe. Thus "actual occasion" refers to a finite reality. "Actual entity," on the other hand, is not so limited. God is understood to be nontemporal in respect to the primordial nature; therefore, God is always referred to as an actual entity, and never as an actual occasion.

Concrescence. This refers to the activity of becoming; it is the unification of many feelings into the single actual entity or occasion. In concrescence, feelings are contrasted and evaluated until they are integrated into a final unity, called the "satisfaction." The activity of concrescence is the self-production of the subject.

---

*This glossary is adapted from one appearing in *God–Christ–Church: A Practical Guide to Process Theology* (New York: Crossroad, 1982), pp. 225–27.

Consequent Nature. Whitehead refers to the physical pole in God as God's consequent nature. This is God's feelings of the world. It is "consequent" in a twofold sense. First, it follows from the primordial nature in God, and second, it follows from the actual happenings in the world.

Creativity. "Creativity," "many," and "one" belong to what Whitehead calls the "category of the ultimate." Every actuality is an instantiation of creativity, or the process whereby many feelings are unified into one determinate subject. In Whitehead, creativity proceeds in two forms: concrescent creativity is the process of becoming, and transitional creativity is the process of influencing another's becoming. In this work, creativity as enjoyment is posited as a third form in order to account for the generation of transitional creativity from the satisfaction of the actuality.

Eternal Objects. These are potentialities for becoming, or forms of definiteness that exist only as possibilities. Their locus is the primordial nature of God.

Immediacy. Often called "subjective immediacy," this refers to the entity's own experience of itself in the concrescent process.

Initial Aim. This inaugurates the becoming of the new occasion; the aim originates in God. From the point of view of God, God's knowledge of the becoming occasion's entire past is integrated with God's own purposes. This yields a particular possibility for what the new occasion might become. Through God's transitional creativity, this possibility is given to the occasion as its initial aim. It provides the occasion with an optimum way of unifying the many influences the occasion receives from its past.

Mental Pole. Every actuality entity has both a mental and a physical pole. The mental pole is the grasp of possibilities relative to the subject's own becoming. This grasp of possibilities guides the entity's integration of feelings from the physical pole into subjective unity.

Negative Prehensions. Every item in the universe is felt; these feelings are called "prehensions." A negative feeling is one in which the particular item felt is excluded from positive integration within the concrescent process.

Objective Immortality. Every actual occasion affects every successor. The effect is the transmission of its own value to another by way of transitional creativity. There can be both repetitive and transformative elements in objective immortality. All entities demand a measure of conformity to themselves, or an accounting of their own particular value in the universe. The more complex entities, however, can also anticipate their own participation in some wider scheme of things, and hence become a force for transformation through objective immortality. The process is objective, since no finite occasion can prehend another in its entirety. Hence the other is felt as object. This process is termed immortality, since it perpetuates one's continuing effect throughout the universe.

Physical Pole. This is the means by which a becoming occasion prehends the transitional creativity of the past. Actual occasions originate in the physical pole, whereas God originates in the mental pole.

Prehension. The feeling of others is called "prehension." It is the process of transforming transitional creativity into concrescent creativity. What is "there" is felt "here" through prehension. Positive prehensions are often called "feelings."

Primordial Nature. This is the equivǎlent of the mental pole in God. The primordial nature is God's grasp of all possibilities. This grasp involves an ordering evaluation of possibilities into a harmony that is called the primoridal vision, or primordial envisagement.

Satisfaction. This constitutes the achievement of unity whereby a subject is itself. It is the goal of concrescence, and completes the occasion. Because of the reversal of poles in God, satisfaction in God relates to the primordial vision, and therefore is everlasting in God.

Subjective Aim. The occasion adapts the initial aim to its own becoming. This adaptation becomes the subjective aim, or the occasion's governing purpose as it determines what it shall become.

Subjective Immortality. This is not a category developed by Whitehead. In this work, subjective immortality refers to God's prehension of the entirety of the finite occasion, including its own sense of itself. Subjective immortality is therefore the finite occasion's participation in God.

Subjective Form. Every prehension is felt with a certain positive or negative value from the point of view of the feeling subject. This constitutes "how" the other is felt. The term "mutuality of subjective form" refers to the way in which each feeling conditions all others as the becoming entity contrasts and compares data in the process of unification.

Superject. To be something for oneself necessarily entails being something for others. "Superject" refers to the sense in which an occasion has an effect beyond itself. This is not optional; it is simply a matter of fact. Whitehead underscores this frequently by calling an actual entity a "subject/superject."

Index